Pain on Their Faces

Testimonies on the Paper Mill Strike, Jay, Maine, 1987-1988

Pain on Their Faces

Testimonies on the Paper Mill Strike, Jay, Maine, 1987-1988

by the Jay-Livermore Falls
Working Class History Project,
sponsored by the Jay Foundation

Peter Kellman
Coordinator

The Apex Press
New York

The Jay-Livermore Falls Working Class History Project began in 1994 when 30 participants of the 1987-88 strike against the International Paper Company's Androscoggin mill in Jay, Maine, gathered to put into writing for future generations what the strike meant to them. This book is a product of that work. Royalties from the sale of this book will be used to support the preservation and dissemination of Jay strike material.

The Apex Press is an imprint of the
Council on International and Public Affairs,
777 United Nations Plaza, Suite 3C,
New York, NY 10017 (800/316-2739)

Library of Congress Cataloging-in-Publication Data

Pain on their faces : testimonies on the paper mill strike, Jay, Maine,
1987-1988 / by the Jay-Livermore Falls Working Class History
Project ; sponsored by the Jay Foundation ; Peter Kellman,
coordinator.
    p. cm.
  ISBN 0-945257-96-1 (soft : alk. paper)
  1. International Paper Company Strike, Jay, Me., 1987-1988
—Sources. 2. United Paperworkers International Union. Local 14
(Jay, Me.)—History—Sources. 3. Strikes and lockouts—Paper
industry—Maine—Jay—History—Sources. I. Kellman, Peter,
1946-. II. Jay-Livermore Falls Working Class History Project.
III. Jay Foundation.
HD5325.P332 1987P35 1998   98-25624
331.892'876'0974172—dc21   CIP

Typeset by Peggy Hurley
Cover design by Warren Hurley
Photo by Peter Kellman of mural by Andrea Kantrowitz
above entrance of Local 14 union hall in Jay
Printed in the United States of America

CONTENTS

Pain on Their Faces
is dedicated to the Jay strikers and all those
who put aside personal hardships
and fought for the common good

FOREWORD
Untold Stories

This is a book of secrets. Well, no, not whispers behind a hand. This is what is called by millions the "Untold Story."

The "Untold Story" is a grand epic of heroes fighting oppression, sometimes dying in ugly ways, usually losing their battles, sometimes imprisoned (buried alive). Sometimes just smashed with defamation. The "Untold Story" is a bright panorama of some of the worst atrocities the world has known, sometimes tortures and massacres, other times "terrible" because the oppressors are so subtle and discreet and therefore almost unstoppable. But more heros appear, a continuing shimmering river of heroic lives.

Why are these stories hidden?

Because these oppressions and atrocities and these heroic deeds against the villain and these villains themselves are Americans in America.

Some say the "Untold Story" is the story of "Labor History" and "Labor Present." To me this is a very limited view. As if the only ones in this secret story are people with hammers and work caps punching a time clock. The oppressors have massacred thousands, and imprisoned millions, starved and stole from and shamed and terrorized people in every aspect of their lives— just for being in the way or uncooperative or not "marketable."

Schoolteachers insist we learn to write and keep our hair cut and our hands clean and our grammar perfect and accent-free so we can compete against each other for those "good jobs" out there. Schools rarely (almost never) teach the "Untold Story" since the textbooks (those nice shiny textbooks we are told are so important) and the computer screen materials (oh, those wonderful computers?) are made by those big companies which might be inconvenienced by popular knowledge of "The Untold Story."

Uh, oh . . . when we use our writing skills to tell this story deemed dangerous by some, are we being naughty?

The following pages are written by our friends and neighbors, by our heroes and heroines: Matthew, Gary, Phil, Brent, Joseph, Gloria, Winnie, Russell, Norman, Henry, Judy, Janice, Earl, Bruce, Pauline, Rene, Gary, Ida, Marie, Raymond, Tom, Maurice M., Laurier, Maurice P., Mike, Joe, Jim, Thomas, Phyllis, Joni, F. C., "Anonymous," Pete, Mike, Vinny, Mitch, Debra and Kenneth, Bob, Nookie, Tex, Anonymous Wife of Anonymous Union Member, Roy and Jack.

Okay, so what have we got here? The "American Dream."

The "American Dream" was a PR scam by bankers and their politicians of the late 1800s, a scam to get votes and blur together the concepts of God and Country with Big Business, a scam to fight the one democratic movement America has known, the Populist Movement.

The American Dream, with all its sly promises was a lie. The American dream has shaped our hearts and minds for over a hundred years. The American Dream lives on and on weirdly and abominably. We speak it. It is the opposite of neighborliness and community and tribal values. It is the opposite of democracy. It is about giving up "home"; it is about competition, inequality, "success," hard work without complaint, hard work without questions, "excellence," "potential," performance, honor, obedience, aspirations, lonely aspirations. We believe in the American Dream with words and actions, with lust, but in spite of all those years of American Dream double-think and its Great Progressive Society, are the gentle, friendly, generous, strong people, who are beginning to tell "Our Story" and to ask, "Where in the hell are We, The People in this big dream of selfish success? Why is the big Dad-Mother-God-Big-Business-Government-Thing letting us down? Why does it feel so good when we bite the Hand That Feeds, turning to our own neighbors and friends and family for trust and truth and strength? What is it about a strike that a company doesn't want but seems end- lessly to provoke? What is going on here? Why, when a strike can get so painful, like a civil war, brother against brother!— why is it that as strikers we are, nevertheless, so proud?

—Carolyn Chute
Author of *The Beans of Egypt,
Maine,* and other works

PREFACE
Labor Struggles Do Not Happen in a Vacuum; They Get Played Out on the Stage of History

John Burke, President of the Pulp and Sulphite Workers Union for 48 years (1917-1965), points to the year 1902 as the beginning of collective bargaining between the union and the International Paper Company. On June 16 of that year, the company and the union signed a one-year agreement covering workers in six mills, including the Otis mill in Jay, Maine. In that agreement, Labor Day, Christmas Day, Independence Day and all Sundays were shutdown holidays. If for some reason the mills were to operate on those days, it had to be agreed to by the union first, with workers paid double time. Ironically, 85 years later to the day, on June 16, 1987, workers at the International Paper Company mill in Jay, Maine, began a strike that lasted 16 months in defense of a number of issues, one of which was to keep their one remaining shutdown holiday, Christmas, and another to retain double time pay for Sunday work.

The eight years following the signing of the 1902 contract were rocky ones marred by interunion disputes that the company took full advantage of. But in 1910, the unions got it together and won an important 13-week strike. In fact, the members and leaders used the strike of 1910 to build strong union organizations in the papermill towns. It is important to remember that in 1910 there were no labor laws that gave legal definition to the relationship between labor and management. The relationship was a *power* relationship and workers were not limited to the arena of the bargaining table when it came to exercising that power. For example, in Jay and Livermore Falls from 1910 until 1921, the union was the dominant institution, more important than the company and more important than the church. The union hall was a center of community activity, putting on plays, making sure goods sold in town were union made and, of course, "perfecting their organizations" to deal with the company.

Then in 1921, the large paper corporations led by the International Paper Company provoked a strike involving over 25,000 workers in the unionized pulp and paper mills across the country. When the strike was finally called off in 1926, only a skeleton of the union that workers built during the strike of 1910 remained. The power that organized workers held in their communities was overtaken by the company and the church.

The strike of 1921 was not only over wages; it was a strike about who would run the community and who would ultimately run the country. This was a strike that took place in the year that Saco and Vanzetti were jailed. That same year 10,000 armed miners marched on West Virginia to free company-run mining towns, but the miners were turned around by Federal troops. Also, in 1921, Eugene Debs and 48 members of the militant union, the Industrial Workers of the World, were doing time in federal prison for union activity. Meanwhile, United States Attorney General Palmer was prosecuting foreign-born, pro-union, politically active American citizens by jailing some and extraditing others. Labor and its allies were taking a big hit and the worker organizations in the pulp and paper mills were no exception.

After the defeat of the unions in Jay and Livermore Falls, the company-built community center, Murray Hall, took the place of the union hall in town and things stayed pretty quiet. If you can call suffering in silence being quiet. In the early 1930s, labor began to stir again and a new labor movement emerged, spearheaded by the Congress of Industrial Organizations, the CIO. However, the weak national unions in the paper industry that survived the strike of 1921 did not embrace the CIO. Instead, they joined with the paper corporations to keep the militant CIO out of the paper mills.

The CIO unions fought to organize enough workers in an industry so the corporations could not force workers to compete against each other in a never ending spiral of lower wages and poorer working conditions. The power of the CIO forced corporations to share more of the wealth the workers created with the people who created the wealth. Thus, if a corporation wanted to increase profit, it had to do it by selling more goods or making the product more efficiently and not by cutting workers' wages or benefits.

After the Second World War, organized American workers, led by the AFL and the CIO, settled into the role of labor as defined in the process called industrial/labor relations. With the acceptance of this role, labor organizations did not challenge the right of the big corporations to direct the society, as they had in the past. The big corporations in return recognized the legal right of unions to represent hourly paid workers as their collective bargaining agents. Labor thought the relationship was permanent.

But the success of the CIO unions in obtaining better wages and working conditions eventually led to a complacency among the unions and their members, and by the late 1970s the unions ability to attract new members and mobilize support for union issues had declined dramatically. Meanwhile, the corporations continued to accumulate more and more wealth and power during this period, becoming more and more disrespectful of workers' rights. The power big corporations held at this point was demonstrated by the election of Ronald Reagan to the Presidency in 1980. Reagan provoked the nation's air traffic controllers, PATCO, into a strike and then proceeded to permanently replace them all. In the private sector, this pattern was perfected by the Phelps Dodge Corporation, with its defeat of the United Steelworkers Union in the Great Arizona Mine Strike of 1983. Since then, it has been repeated hundreds of times in mills, mines and factories all over the country, where workers have lost jobs trying to defend the right to bargain collectively. This devastation to workers and communities moved closer to home in 1986 when the Boise Cascade Company forced a strike in Rumford, Maine, permanently replacing 347 paper mill workers before the union called the strike off.

The International Paper Company, the largest paper company in the world and the largest private landowner in the United States, led the paper industry in the 1980s the way it did in the 1920s. It forced a strike. International Paper began the process by first gaining concessions from workers in its smaller mills in the early 1980s, and then at the larger mills, by pleading they were needed to upgrade the mills to be competitive. Finally, in the fall of 1986, Paul O'Neil, International Paper Company's President, was dispatched to western Maine to spread the word that the company still wanted more concessions and was serious about making profits by cutting wages. O'Neil laid out the company's demands: the end of double time pay for Sunday work (production workers were required to work 39 Sundays a year); elimination of the only remaining holiday when the mill shut down, Christmas; elimination of 350 union jobs by sub-contracting all maintenance work; and deletion of 170 jobs through a program the company called Project Productivity. The company also wanted the Town of Jay to cut the mills property tax rate. To top it off, the company wanted less environmental regulations and a decrease in Workers Compensation rates from the state. While the company was making these concessionary demands on mill workers and communities, it was making huge profits and giving its executives big raises.

The "fight back" began in March of 1987 when workers at the International Paper Company mill in Mobile, Alabama, rejected a concessionary contract proposal. The company responded by locking out all 1,400 union workers. In June, workers at three other International Paper Company mills voted against concessionary proposals and supported their locked out sisters and brothers in Mobile by "hitting the bricks" in Lockhaven, Pennsylvania, De Pere, Wisconsin, and Jay, Maine.

The struggle in the three struck mill towns went on for 16 months, with Jay workers leading the way. Workers in Jay took political power in town. They passed an unprecedented environmental ordinance, elected their own people to positions of power and increased the property assessment on the mill by $100 million. In 1988, the Maine press voted the Jay strike the number one story in the state. The strike was covered in the magazine section of the *New York Times*, 40 articles were written about the strike in the *Boston Globe*, the *Lewiston Sun* published close to 1,000 articles on the strike, and television stations in Boston and Maine produced documentaries about the struggle in Jay.

This activity on the part of the press was in response to the union's program. The union held a weekly mass meeting, open to the public and regularly attended by a thousand or more people. The union organized a caravan which toured New England, spreading the story of the struggle to cities, towns, schools, plant gates, legislatures, main streets and union halls along the way. Mass demonstrations were held in Jay, the largest of which attracted over 10,000 people. The local union spearheaded striker replacement legislation in the U.S. Congress and the Maine state legislature. The role of the local union in supporting Jesse Jackson's campaign for President contributed to his strong finish in the Maine primary and thus proving that Jackson was a viable candidate in both white and black America.

The community of striking families in Jay grew and changed. People found a life based on friendship and solidarity preferable to a life centered on the International Paper Company. It was a life supported by an extended family that included people from Poland to Nicaragua and Australia to Sweden who traveled to Jay to lend the struggle a hand. As time wore on, people began to sense it was going to take more than a three-mill strike to beat the International Paper Company. It was going to take a new labor movement. But the idea that these paper mill workers could or should lead a new movement was not held by the leadership of the national union. The strikes were called off by the national union on October 10, 1988, stranding 2,100 workers who had been permanently replaced by the International Paper Company, and put the new movement for justice in the paper mill towns on hold.

Meanwhile, what of the people who conducted this strike? We know very little of what the paper mill strikes of 1908, 1910 and 1921 meant to the people who walked the picket lines, organized the mass meetings and lost the pay checks. Historians interpret past events, but there is seldom a record of the voices of those who actually participated in labor struggles.

This book was put together to assure that the descendants

of this struggle will know, in some small part, what the participants of this struggle did not know about the previous struggles.
And so we leave for the union warriors of the future, in our
own words, what the strike of 1987-88 in Jay, Maine, meant to
us . . . the tears . . . the pain . . . the excitement . . . the betrayal
. . . the happiness and, most importantly, the hope and solidarity, *uncensored* in our own words.

—Peter Kellman
Coordinator of the Jay-Livermore
Falls Working Class History Project

Acknowledgments

We would like to acknowledge everyone who contributed to the struggle for worker's rights in Jay, Maine, during the strike against the International Paper Company in 1987-88. For many, the task was too painful and they did not write. The essays of those who did write created this book.

The Jay-Livermore Falls Working Class History Project would also like to acknowledge and thank the following people and organizations that contributed to the project:

Bates College
Haymarket Peoples Fund
Pine Tree Folk School
Resist Foundation
Claire Duguay
Jon Falk
Professor John Hinshaw
Casey McGuire
The law firm of McTeague, Higbee
Jeffrey Young

And, of course, Local 14 of Jay

TESTIMONIES

A Ballot for the Future

Matthew J. Martin (4 & 5 Machines)
1987

The mill-labor trend over the last few years is finally hitting home. Around 1,200 union jobs are in limbo this week at International Paper Company's Androscoggin mill in Jay, Maine.

As a papermaker and a union member, I am bound to work under the provisions of the labor contract between IP Company and the United Paperworkers International Union (UPIU Locals 246 and 14). But when there is no agreement, there is no work. That causes me to worry about my livelihood and that of my family's.

Having worked just over one year in the mill, the immediate impact of a lost income will be hardfelt by persons such as me. If I cannot compensate for the wages lost during a dispute, I may be forced to give up the possessions I have waited so long to gain: my home, my car, but most of all my pride and independence. Those things I won't give up, not without a fight.

You might say this is just another sob story, well, indeed, it is. But what is not realized is that we all should be crying. There has been a stranglehold placed on the necks that carry this nation. American organized labor is dying. We've seen it in the steel industry, trucking, coal mining, auto manufacturing, railroads, housing, papermaking—and the list goes on.

1

But, worst of all, we see it in the unemployment lines, in the eyes of the hungry and homeless. How much deeper can we allow the rift to grow? Will we be able to stop it before it undermines medicine, education or even the constitution that sets us apart from all nations? I fear not, and for my children more than for myself. They will inherit what remains.

For my children, I must stand up to the money-hungry corporate giants and the union-busting administration that lets them run rampant. On June the 4th, 1987, I will be voting my conscience as the American worker that I am. I will be joined by the labor forces of four other IP mills who have pooled their votes across the nation. We are standing united against management, not so much for no Sunday premium pay, or no holidays or because the company [is trying] to intimidate us with their final offer, no-budge bargaining, . . . [but so] our children won't be working under the same sweatshop conditions that called for organized labor in the first place.

Young supporter speaking into mike, with Local 14 president Bill Meserve, at a mass meeting. Photo by Rene Brochu.

To the Board of Directors, International Paper Company

Gary Desjardins
1988

Dear Board Member:

As the IP strike passes its one-year anniversary, I have some reflections that I would like to share with you. First of all, the Andro mill, which sits alongside the Androscoggin River in the Androscoggin Valley, was built in this location because the company's original mill—namely, Otis—was built around the turn of the century. Before the strike, there were some third- and fourth-generation descendants of the original employees of the Otis working within the Andro mill. One of the reasons that the Andro mill was built in this area was due to the supply of dedicated and experienced paper workers. I, myself, have 22 years of service, my father has 27 and my grandfather had 52 years of service upon his retirement. There were three languages spoken in this area: French, English and "Papermaking." IP was looked upon as the number one company in this area, providing good, stable jobs for its dedicated employees, and had a good reputation with the town of Jay and the Jay school system.

All of this has taken a complete turn-around, and IP is now looked down upon with great disfavor. All due to John Georges' insatiable greed, and his total disrespect for those dedicated employees who helped make this company number one. This was all endorsed by you—and the other board members. The management of a company is evaluated by its ability to get its employees to meet, or exceed, production levels, to avoid accidents, to reduce employee turnover and to build enthusiasm so that employees will take pride in the company and tell others. IP has failed miserably in all of these areas; and for what? The profit that was lost due to the strike is astronomical! What price can you put on a company's reputation? A company is what its employees have made it, and that is the "bottom line." So-called educated individuals, such as yourselves who have decided to make war with its employees, are foolhardy, at best. You can have all of the education that is available, but without common sense it is useless, and this strike brings this statement home.

The "union-busting" tactics that IP has taken upon itself, which can cause the loss of employees with 20, 30 and 40 years of experience to end up with "scabs" who are inexperienced and are like jackals with no morals, is insane for a company that is so viable. If you had the choice of an experienced physician or someone fresh out of medical school for a major operation on yourself or your family, *who would you choose?* The list goes on! Common sense tells us that there is no substitute for experience! (Unless, of course, if you are IP, with its blind goal to rid the company of unions, no matter what the cost.) The "whiz-kid" mentality that has taken over this company, with the ideology that [its present] course should be set for the long run, is *correct.* But not for more profit and longevity—[instead] for internal strife, and [for] a company whose reputation will be damaged for generations to come.

Our message is spreading further every day, and if you don't realize that, then you must be living in a vacuum. Several of my striking co-workers who have found work at other jobs, some of them at other paper companies, have been well received. They have received accolades, and have been told that they cannot believe that a company like IP would let experienced people go. Some employers have told them they are sorry that they cannot afford to pay them more, for they are certainly worth it. Also, a few of them have been immediately hired into supervisory status.

It is unfortunate that no one on the IP Board seemingly has enough "moral fiber" to stand up to John Georges, and end this futile battle that is like a "cancer" and, in time, will undoubtedly consume a once proud company. All because of the narrow-mindedness of one individual, namely, John Georges. A teacher once told me, "dare to be different," and I say the same to you. Stand up to John Georges, because some day soon the facts will be made known as to the cost of the strikes and lockout. I do not think that present and future stockholders will be impressed. Then, they will look to you, the policy makers, for answers. Do you have them? Can you justify the hundreds of millions of dollars that it has cost in lost production, customers and expenses incurred that otherwise would have been *profit*. How many more price increases can you make to justify your current profit? There will be a day of reckoning, and I feel that it will be here soon, sooner than you think. Talk to another board member—he or she may be wanting to talk to you. Show some backbone, and question Georges on his goal for the future of IP—NOW!

> Sincerely yours,
> Gary Desjardins, a third-generation
> paper maker, with 22 years experience
> at the Jay location. (Now happily
> employed as a broker realtor!)
> Thank you, and have a good day.

Mark Well that in This Place You Stood

Phil Edwards

Brothers and sisters, family members, friends of labor:

My father built bridges under fire in France in World War I and my brother died in a B-17 over England in World War II. I landed on a beach in North Korea in 1950, and, oh, the country and the government were behind us in those days. But in 1987, in Jay, Maine, we had a war about corporate greed and the depredation of worker's rights and where then was the country and where then was the government? Did the governor of the state or the President of the United States stand up to corporate America? They did, in fact, encourage the pillaging of worker's hard-earned benefits. Where was the United States Congress? Where was the national media during our struggle?

What does the International Executive Board think is the important issue here? Are they concerned that they will deplete their funds? I tell you, they should have been ready to sell everything they owned to win this conflict. Are working people anywhere naive enough to think this is not their work?

To those of you who helped, and your numbers are legion, I give my thanks, my most earnest heartfelt thanks, but to those who did not, I would paraphrase John Donne, "ask not for whom the bell tolls. It tolls for thee."

Sisters and brothers, I do not have the words to ease your pain on this sorry occasion. Each of you have given of your time, your energy and your personal fortune to advance the cause of

6

labor during this dark age. History will record that you, like the embattled farmers at Concord Bridge, fired a shot heard 'round the world. Do not despair that the battle was lost along another front. *Mark well that in this place you stood,* shoulder to shoulder, faced the enemy and did not flinch nor bow down.

I have known some of you for most of the 30-odd years that I have worked at International Paper. I have found you to be honest tradesmen, in the Maine tradition. Since the strike began, I have come to realize how much I value your friendship. I have seen lambs become lions and sparrows become eagles. From your ranks have emerged salesmen and lawyers, organizers and orators.

You have been tempered into steel in the crucible of war, and you will never again be as you were before.

I could not allow this moment to pass without telling you, how proud my wife and I are to have soldiered with you.

"Stop Corporate Greed" street march, Boston, winter, 1988.

The More Involved I Got, the Better I Felt

Brent Gay

On the last night before the strike began (June 15, 1987), I was working the 3 to 11 shift. When I walked out the gate at the end of the shift I had a large knot in my stomach. There was no foretelling the sick feelings of not knowing what was going to happen from then on, or if I would ever be back. It was the most empty feeling I ever had.

On June 16, I went to Augusta for a labor demonstration at the capitol, the first I was ever involved with but not to be the last.

In the next few days, I was at the mill along with a few hundred other strikers. We blocked the road and caused all kinds of disruptions. When the scabs started arriving there was mob violence, smashing windshields, kicking in fenders, etc., and I was in the middle of it and not minding it a bit. Maybe even enjoying it. At one point, I chased a Wackenhut guard down the railroad tracks, screaming and trying to start a fight. I remember hearing Terri saying, "Is that really Dad?" This was only the beginning of developing a hate for scabs and IP that I never knew I was capable of. On one occasion, at T&J Store a BE&K [a construction company in Birmingham, Alabama, notorious for crossing picket lines to do maintenance and construction work] worker came in and I made comments that could have provoked a fight. Celina and others thought there was going to be one. At that point, I had developed enough hate the thought of a fight

8

didn't bother me, even though normally that is the last thing in the world I would get into. When people said they thought there was going to be a fight, I replied I had the advantage because I had built up so much hate I really wanted to hurt him. He left the store in a hurry.

I started picketing at the main gate, screaming and cursing the scabs each day until it was tearing at my gut so much I started doing my picket duty on the railroad track. This helped for a while, but soon I was looking for a way to be more involved. Since my future was at stake here, I wanted to do whatever possible to make the strike a success. This was the beginning of becoming more involved, and I guess at times too involved. *The more involved I got, the better I felt,* like I was having a positive effect, not just letting someone else deal with the future. It was what I could do to help control my own destiny.

There were many good times and gatherings at the hall. Whole families felt comfortable being a part of it and it helped build relationships. There were times there were tears. I spent most every day at the hall; I couldn't be away from the activity.

My increased involvement started with becoming a picket captain, manning the picket trailer and then quickly volunteering to go to other locals to speak. As much as I hated to stand in front of people to talk, I really wanted to do it. My first engagement was a IBEW local in Augusta. My knees were shaking and I was scared to death. It got easier and I started enjoying it. I spoke at union meetings, schools, colleges and civic groups. I took over Project D, our title for the speakers program, and was scheduling people all over the country for speaking engagements. It grew so much, I was no longer calling to ask to send someone—I could hardly keep up with requests that came in. There were even requests from presidential candidates to come and speak to us. I testified before legislature committees on a couple of occasions. I never dreamed I would ever do that or speak to college classes. I always hated to talk on the phone and call strangers. After a while I would call "anybody anywhere" without a second thought. I was always on the phone.

On August 3rd, 1987, a rally was held and a march on the mill. It was an experience to remember—7,000 to 10,000 people (it depends on who was counting) converged on the main gate.

The line stretched a mile. People just kept on coming and coming. I couldn't get over the sight.

In November of 1987, another march on the mill was held. When we arrived, someone unfolded a homemade rebel flag from the digester. The crowd went wild and wanted to storm the gate. I was a marshal and was supposed to help keep things under control. My heart wasn't in it. I really wanted to see the crowd take the gate and bust some heads.

There were two things that always kept me going. The Wednesday night meetings where 2,000 to 3,000 people attended each week. It was like a big family come together for support. When they all started clapping and stomping, spirits got lifted and stirred excitement. The union hall was the place to go when you were down. It not only became a gathering place to get together; it was the place where things were always happening. It was the center for everything.

October 10, 1988, was probably the worst day during the strike. All officers and committee people were called to come to the hall. When we arrived, we were told that at a meeting in Nashville the strike was called off because of lack of support from other IP locations and money. It was over and we lost! Just like that. I saw grown men cry, including myself. It was the same as when a close family member dies suddenly. Everything we worked so hard for in 16 months was over and we hadn't won anything. The only way to describe the day is it was a wake, with families gathering at the hall to console each other. The news media swarmed to report the death. They were disappointed. No one had regrets and were not ready to give up. I never left the hall that day until almost midnight. Families and supporters came from all over to be with us when they heard the news.

It was at this point we had to explain to other locals what had happened and the fight wasn't over. Some wanted to take on the UPIU for not enough support. I talked to locals and wrote a letter to the [UPIU] "Paperworker" newspaper that, even though the legal strike was over, I felt "strike" was an attitude and I was still on strike and the fight was not over.

The local then entered into negotiations with IP to obtain a recall agreement to get people back to work as jobs opened up.

Everybody had been replaced at this time. It took over five months to finalize it. The management people showed their dislike for the strikers and created more hate. It became very evident and frustrating how much they wanted to break us. I became more stubborn and determined to get them any way possible. They were the enemy and they were going to pay.

In June 1989, I was one of the delegates to the pension negotiations in Memphis. On the first day, all the delegates stood and stated their names and locals. When it was my turn, I stated my name and said "Local 14." IP negotiators whose backs were to us spun around to look. It felt great. I felt everything we had done made them sit up and take notice and we were not beaten yet.

I had received my recall letter and would be returning to work on July 7. On the plane home from the negotiations, K.C. Lavoie asked me how it felt to be returning to the mill. My reply was: "Not very good, going back to mill full of fucking scabs." He walked off and left me alone.

When I did return to work, I hated scabs so much and many of the salaried people, my stomach was always in knots and I couldn't eat for weeks. There were days I was so agitated I didn't go to work. To this day, there is still salaried people favoring scabs, which keeps us always fighting for our rights.

The recertification vote finally was held the summer of '92 after holding it off since November 1987. In an effort to keep the union in the mill, it was necessary to represent scabs and try to convince them the union was needed. This took a lot of pride-swallowing, but I did it. It upset the company when a scab would listen to me and sided with the union. This felt great, still beating the company in small ways. I thought we had a small chance to win the election—300 union to 800 scabs.

When the vote was counted we had lost 2 to 1. This day was as bad as the day the strike was called off. Again, people gathered at the hall to be with each other and curse the scabs. Some got drunk, some cried. I did a little of both.

If there is any consolation at all, it is the fact IP couldn't break my spirit (even though they might have come close). We took them on and I don't think they ever expected to come up against such determination and organization. We may have lost the war, but IP knows it was in a fight and losses are beyond calculation. Spoils to the victor.

In just a few years, I have done and felt things I probably never would have in a lifetime. I think, as a family, we are closer and our values have changed. Only a struggle like this can pull you together or break you apart. There were a lot more good times than bad, times I will remember the rest of my life. I never regretted going on strike, for I always had my pride.

Rally at State House in Augusta, June 16, 1987. Photo by Rene Brochu.

Christmas Is for Church and Family

Joseph Shink

On June 16, 1987, at 7 A.M., we the people of Local #14 went on strike against IP Company. My reasons for doing this were: 1) the company wanted to eliminate about 250 jobs in maintenance, oilers, custodians, some yard or utility jobs. If I voted to accept that offer, I was putting one of my brothers out of work; 2) I would have been forced to work Christmas day. I think *Christmas is for church and family;* 3) we stood to lose all time and a half, and double for working over eight hours, Sundays and holidays. Then came "team concept" where you had to learn all jobs in a department, which we already had by learning the job ahead.

It was the first time in my life that I didn't have a job to go to. It was scary, but with the help of each other and family it was possible to keep going. We had good support from all walks of life—other paper workers, postal workers and organizations. Then after a few months, we were all fired and replaced permanently by scabs. How I hate them. The older I get, the more I hate them. The picket line made me sick to my stomach so I used to work the phones in the union hall and did some roving, bringing the picketers coffee and donuts. I also did some weekend traveling to talk to supporters to let them know how things were going, and also to raise money for the cause. If I had to do it again, I would do the same thing all over again.

13

Union Family

Gloria Poulin

When the strike first started, being the wife of a striker I thought, "This has nothing to do with me and it won't last long. Wouldn't a company that had its beginnings right here in this community appreciate the dedication of generation after generation of hard workers?" Wrong!

One night, while walking the picket line with my husband and friends and seeing all those trailers lined up in clear view of the picket line, I got angry. This is all so unfair and clearly premeditated. I asked my husband what I could do to help? He said maybe they could use my help at the union hall, so that's where I spent a great deal of my time, from then on making phone calls, stamping envelopes and copying materials for media packets. Every day, I thought to myself, "What more can we do; we're right and right always wins eventually." Isn't that how it's supposed to work? Maybe in half-hour sitcoms and fairy tales.

The most memorable event for me was the Amtrak train trip to Denver to attend the shareholders meeting. My husband and I had to roll up all the change we had been saving over the years so that I could buy my ticket to go. There were 37 of us, no one with much money. In fact, we had all brought food with us, knowing we couldn't afford the dining car for all our meals. We had a regular smorgasbord in our car. We all shared with each other what we had brought. Maybe there was one exception—

one of our group had brought a whole loaf of peanut butter and jam sandwiches. When I see her to this day, we still have a laugh over her sandwiches!

Starting out the trip, I was a little apprehensive. Denver is a long way away. A three-day trip on a train with 36 other men and women, most of whom I didn't know real well. From the git-go, I had nothing to worry about. We all stayed together and watched out for each other, from getting on the "Green-line" to get to the train station, to watching each others' luggage, and to sharing our food, books and tapes.

Right before we arrived at the Chicago station, where we had a lay-over before we could board the train for Denver, my best friend broke her glasses. All the men and women in our group scrambled all over that station looking for super glue or anything they could find to effect a repair on her glasses. One man, dear soul, was even puffing on his cigar extra hard, in an attempt to get it hot enough to try to fuse the plastic on the glasses together. It didn't work, but he did try. They even offered to take up a collection to pay for new glasses when we arrived in Denver. She said it wasn't necessary, she had a credit card.

On the train, most of us wore our blue "striker" tee shirts. These caused a lot of travelers to ask about the strike, giving each one of us an opportunity to state our case, spreading our message. Only, one woman aboard thought we were all part of a bowling team.

The day of the meeting, I'm wondering how we will do. No need to worry. The women all looked their very best and the men shed their tee shirts and arrived at the meeting wearing their best suits and ties. The ones that spoke at the meeting were very articulate and straight-forward, stating the case that this unfair strike was costing the shareholders a lot of money, and needless hardship to a lot of decent hard-working people.

Our trip home was long and tiresome. We all wondered if it did any good. Maybe. At least we had spread our message further to the people of Colorado in the press. Can't hurt.

My own feeling about the trip was I had found family. These people were truly brothers and sisters dealing with a shared pain and caring for each other. I don't know if my going made any difference in the long run, but I'm glad I went. It's a trip I'll remember the rest of my life. Gave me a better perspective on the "Union" family. They are truly a family; with a common goal: better working conditions for each and every one of us.

Pickets on sidewalk at International Paper Annual Meeting, Denver, Colorado, May 10, 1988.

Pain on Their Faces

Winnie Shink

When the famous strike of International Paper Company started on June 16, 1987, I had no intention of getting involved. Then one evening I decided to go to the end of the bridge where a nightly vigil was held. When I saw the hurt and *pain on the faces* of those attending every time a scab crossed that bridge to steal their jobs, something just struck me inside. From that moment on, it seemed like there just wasn't enough I could do to help. But I would do my best, not only for my husband and his two brothers who were out of work, but for their relatives and friends as well.

Many hours were spent on the picket line—caravans to different states, leafleting, food bank, clothing bank and whatever else was needed around the union hall. Also those life-saving meetings every Wednesday evening with supporters from all over the world coming to our community building to help boost our morale. How we miss those meetings and friendships! I'm not sorry for one minute that I spent, thinking that in some small way I was helping out, and I would do it all over again.

As for the way it changed my life, it made me much more outspoken (which can be good or bad) and more independent. I'm also very hesitant about speaking to strangers for fear they may be a scab. My feelings about them *were* very strong during the strike and they have not and will never change for as long as I live.

17

Although we were taught never to hate anyone, when those scabs went into the mill, the word hate took on a new meaning for me—and that is what my feelings will always be for them.

IP Pig on picket sign. Photo by Ed Slick.

It Made Your Blood Thicken

Russell Brackett

On June 17, 1987, I stood outside the IP fence watching scabs going in the gate at the mill taking our jobs, due to IP being too proud to bargain with the union. It was two years and two months before I went back through those gates.

In the meantime, it was hard for me to stand on the picket lines in the hot and cold weather watching those scabs laugh their way in. I took my turn on the lines and at the food bank, which was a big help to everybody. The food was a godsend. I also took bus trips with the rest of the people and my wife, trying to win the awful fight that IP made.

It was hard at 55 years of age to find a job, being a striker and not knowing how long the strike was going to last. It was horrible. *It made your blood thicken.* My wife and I did get into Forsters. We were lucky—we got the 11 to 7 shift for ten months.

Then one day in August I got a letter from IP. They wanted me back. What a change when I went back—I could hardly take it. I had my old job back again and stayed for five years. Thank God.

We Were Forced to Go On Strike

Norman J. Ouellette

My name is Norman J. Ouellette and I was born in Chisholm, Maine, on February 26, 1931. I have been a life-long resident in the town of Jay. I graduated from Jay high school in 1950 and went to work for International Paper in June of the same year. I worked for the company until June 16, 1987, when *we were forced to go on strike* against the company. I was a machine tender at the time of the labor dispute and this was the highest paying hourly job in the whole complex.

This strike of 1987 is just a repetition of the other strikes that happened in the town of Jay beginning in 1908.

My roots go back more than a hundred years in this area. My grandfather, Charles Ouellette, was involved in the construction of the first paper mill in Jay. This is where International Paper Company started the company. In the strike of 1921, my grandfather and my father both lost their jobs as a result of this strike. My grandfather never went back to the company, but after being out for six years, my father returned to work for IP until he was 65 years old. My father was born in 1898 on Main Street in Chisholm, the first [child] born in Chisholm. He had older brothers and sisters that were born in Gilbertville, and [the rest in Jay] down by the river, close to the railroad bridge.

Prior to the construction of International Paper's first mill and prior to having people reside in Chisholm, my grandparents lived in Gilbertville until that small town burned down.

After the fire, homes were built alongside the river and eventually these homes also burned down. Homes were then built on main street in Chisholm that are still standing today. IP has had a bad reputation over the years, as is still evident today. It is certainly time that the people were made aware of IP's irresponsibility.

Working Class History

After the strike ended on October 10, 1988, my anger and frustration of the strike were directed toward the company and the International Union president and his board of directors. I knew that there are a lot of people out there who are hungry and would not have any problem going to work for the company. I was not surprised we lost the strike because the company was so large.

Even today my anger is increasing, not because of the scabs but because of the way our government is functioning. When you have a minority in the U.S. Senate controlling bills through filibusters, and especially the Republicans working for the corporations, the American people do not have a chance. The legal system is corrupt as it can be. The Senators, instead of representing their constituents, control them.

There is so much propaganda on television and the newspapers.

The majority of the people are working for low wages, doing all they can to make ends meet, and consequently do not have the time and energy to find out what is really happening in Washington.

What I have learned, and what I am still learning from all this, is that unless all the unions in this country merge into one large union and become serious about helping the workers, there is not much hope for a long, long time.

This is what we all should be writing about and teaching and striving for.

A good example of the people who are in control is the fact that they will not allow any of this work being produced [on the history project] to get into the school systems.

I Took a Stand

Henry Lerette

Before the strike, I had served the union as a shop steward and as an area vice president. During the strike, I wanted to remain active in some way. I did my share of picket line duty, but I needed to do more. I felt that I could best help by going to other places to explain to others our reason for going on strike.

I traveled to cities and town from Madawaska, Maine, to Plymouth, Massachusetts. For me it was a great experience that I really enjoyed. Usually I was accompanied by another member. We spoke to other unions, clubs, college students, citizens, etc. We were treated very well everywhere we went. I remember the time I went to Plymouth, Massachusetts, to address a group of union carpenters. I expected to see the usual 10 to 20 members at the meeting, but when I entered the hall, there were about 300 people attending a business meeting. I nearly panicked. I guess I did alright, but it was scary at the time. Another time at a meeting of clothing workers, I got the feeling that they weren't very sympathetic to our cause, perhaps because of our higher wages.

I guess the trip I remember the most vividly was when three of us went to Manchester, New Hampshire. On the way down the turnpike, as we passed a Burger King, an 18 wheeler with International Paper lettering on the side was entering the highway. As we passed him, one of my companions flipped the driver the bird. We thought it was funny. A few miles down the road we came upon another semi with IP on it. As I started to pass he pulled over into the passing lane. I pulled back, he pulled back. I pulled out, he pulled out. Then I noticed the other semi come up behind us. That has to be the most uncomfortable sandwich I've ever been in. I doubt that the semi drivers even knew why they got the bird.

All in all I have some really nice memories from the strike. Many new friends and acquaintances. Truly an experience to remember. Most of all, *I took a stand* for what I believed in and have no regrets.

Goose Bumps

Judy (Billings)Willett

- The grateful looks and heartfelt thanks from the members of Locals 14 and 246 as they were presented with the many checks, donations and job offers from fellow union brothers and sisters.
- The many trips to Jay for your mass meetings month, after month, after month.
- The many friends and people that I met while attending your mass meetings.
- The *goose bumps* that I felt and still feel every time I hear "that song" (the union makes us strong!)
- The horns, bells, sirens and shouts on the many "trips around the mill."
- The determination that I saw on the many faces, "we're gonna win this one!"
- The disappointment and heartache that I felt along with everyone else when we were told at the last meeting, "the strike is ended!"
- But, for me, the best memory of the IP strike of 1987 was meeting the "Love of my Life" as a result of it: Gary Willett, who married me July 6, 1991!

Recording Secretary
Local 900 UPIU
Rumford, ME

The Strike Was Not Lost in Jay

Joan Fuller

The biggest reason I became involved with the strike of 1987 was because my husband, Earl Fuller, and my son, Eric Fuller, were strikers. I probably would have been involved anyway, as my maternal grandfather, Ted Ragan, a blacksmith, and my father, J. Henry Croson, a papermaker, were both involved with the strikes of 1910 and 1921. I also participated in a teacher strike in 1978 in Jay. We walked off the job contrary to Maine state law. It was not a popular issue, but we got a good contract. There were teacher scabs who crossed our line.

After 66 years, who would have dreamed that International Paper Company could treat their loyal and committed workers in such a callous and heartless manner? Live and learn!

The first year, Earl was gone on caravans more that he was home. When he was at home, we both picketed. We put up many, many guests at our home for meals and sleeping quarters. We were uneasy about some socialist and communist people who became involved from the Boston area. We both are strong adherents to the democratic process.

I received criticism and a few threatening phone calls, as I was a teacher in Jay at the time. I also received special consideration and respect from those who counted. The children of strikers were confused and upset. They knew I was sympathetic. Most of the Jay Teacher's Association was supportive with funding and consideration. Luckily scab kids were few and far between.

The Wednesday night rallies were a time of high emotion and great brotherhood when supporters from far and near gathered. I cannot bear to hear "Solidarity Forever" without crying.

The strike was not lost in Jay, Maine. The upper union echelon let Local 14 down. I hope there is a higher power that will someday make them pay their just dues. Until there is better leadership in top union management, there is little hope for better conditions.

Mass meeting in Jay Community Center, October 12, 1987. Photo by Rene Brochu.

We Fought Hard

Janice Brackett

It was horrible. I had to work two jobs to help keep things going. Hope I don't see another strike like it. I worked every week at the food bank. We handled a lot of food for the people. At the beginning of the strike, I was on the picket line as often as I could be, no matter what the weather was, but we were there for a good reason.

I went on bus trips and caravans near and far and *we fought hard.* I attended every weekly meeting. It was hard on the picket lines to see those scabs going in and taking our husbands' jobs.

This was all due to IP being greedy.

Our Local Won the Strike

Earl Fuller

I am a worker—not a writer! I started work in 1943 for 43 cents an hour. There was a lot that was not right with working conditions. Every union meeting, problems were worked out gradually. Not perfect, but improvement was made.

As time went on, my union helped me with finances, pension benefits, vacations and on and on. When someone uses you good, you stand by them and that is my union.

Now I am retired and my pension money keeps coming in. It is not an IP check. It is a union check. The company never would have had a pension if it were not for good labor unions.

Now for the strike. After I voted to strike, I went back to my job as machine tender on #3 and said to my fellow workers, "Why would anyone in their right mind vote for a strike?" I had everything going for me. But as it was presented to me by my union, so many of my good union brothers and sisters were being replaced by outside contractors, I felt I had to take a stand.

Someday it will have to happen again. I know the scabs are not so dumb. They will wake up someday and go union. We need new blood in the top union leaders. They are worse than the scabs. *Our local won the strike.* It was the bastards at headquarters that did us in. In my opinion, the top union leaders were in cahoots with International Paper. There is never a day when the strike and circumstances do not cross my mind.

A little note: my ex-long and good working friend called

me up and wanted me to be a super scab [union members who crossed the picket line]. He wanted me to join him. And I said, "No way!" Like his father, he also became a super scab. You see we never forget who were scabs and who weren't. Days went by and he called and called. He bellyached and I said, "You made your bed. Lie in it, scab." He has paid one hell of a big price. T.S.

"Scabs steal honest workers' jobs." Photo by Rene Brochu.

I Now Speak Out When I See an Injustice

Bruce J. Stevens

I felt that a strike was the only option that we had because the company did not want to negotiate.

During the first six months of the strike, I did many different shifts of picketing at various gates. By December, though, I could no longer cope with picketing and seeing the replacement workers come and go, knowing that they were doing my job and that of my friends. After four hours of picketing, I would go home depressed with a terrible headache. I then volunteered to do anything to help the local, except picket.

When the local started the Car-A-Van in January of 1988, I eagerly volunteered to participate. I traveled the entire Maine Car-A-Van. At first, I helped with the leafleting and at the rallies that we had along the way. As we progressed, I was drafted to help out with the media committee. At first, I just helped with press releases and getting the reporters to speak to the local's spokesperson. I then became one of the spokespersons for the local. I conducted newspaper interviews and taped radio interviews. As we made our way toward the southern part of the state, I conducted television interviews also. As our travels expanded into other states, I found myself doing live radio talk shows and a live television talk show.

I traveled in Maine, New Hampshire, Vermont, New York, Massachusetts, Pennsylvania, Connecticut and Virginia. I was a member of a delegation made up of members from Jay, Mobile, Lock Haven and De Pere that went to Washington, D.C. to talk to Congressman Joseph Brennan about his strikebreaker bill before he introduced it.

I found, as many of our members did, talents that I did not know I had. The members that ran the various committees, such as the food bank and the job bank, organized the trips, and all the other committees all did an excellent job.

For the first time in my life, I felt that I was actually accomplishing something by traveling for the local, and that I could do something to change the world. I know that going to work to support my family before the strike was important, but by traveling around the country and getting our message out and gaining support for our cause made me feel that I mattered and that I could make a difference and help a lot of people.

When I was not traveling, I would help with the job bank. This was another important function to keep members of the local employed. The job bank resulted in better relations with the trade unions. I also helped with mailings from the hall and do other various tasks.

Sometimes between trips I would get a little down, but then on the next trip I would rediscover that people do care and would help. I met many nice people that would open their homes to you. They provided us with a place to stay, and many with good, home-cooked meals.

My family was very supportive of me during the strike. I think that the strike has made me a better person. I used to see things that were wrong and think that there was nothing that I could do about it. *I now speak out when I see an injustice.* I may not be able to correct it, but at least now I try to do something about it.

Because of the strike, I became involved in local politics and have been elected to the Jay Board of Selectmen three times. I have also been elected three times as Recording Secretary of Local #14.

It Was Their Right to Do So

Pauline Shink

It's too bad the strike had to happen, but it did. *It was their right to do so.* Others go on strike and things work out; ours didn't. It tore families and friendships apart. Homes, cars and properties were damaged. There is still much bitterness in the town.

The ones I feel sorry for were the kids where I worked. So many of them were confused. They didn't know what was going on. They were being picked on by kids whose fathers didn't strike. There was name calling. Some of the strikers' kids defended their fathers by fighting. A lot of the kids were made fun of because of the clothes they wore, so-called hand-me-downs. Kids can be very cruel.

Where I worked, they thought the men were crazy to go [on] strike. The only thing they were afraid of was where the money for their grants was going to come from.

I was proud of each and every one of them. I had family and friends on strike.

As a lot of you notice, the mill isn't doing as good as it did 20 years ago.

The First and Second Split

Rene Castonguay

When the company prepared to build the Androscoggin mill in 1963, the rank and file at the Otis mill were told that the mill would be separate and neither company nor mill seniority would prevail in hiring for the new mill, even though the new mill was in the physical boundaries of the existing mill at Otis. Also, at this time, rumors were rampant that once the new mill was on line, the Otis would be shut down.

Many meetings were held at the old union hall at the fire station and much arguing went on among the rank and file. Somehow the various international reps came into agreement that the company could choose whomever it wanted to man the new mill. Thus, the first split.

At those meetings, and during the hiring, you felt as if you were a player and your coach was coaching both your team and the other team. He would tell you one thing and he would tell them something altogether different.

After the new mill was manned, the rank and file again distanced themselves further from solidarity by voting to end their membership in the northern division, a block of company mills in the northern part of the country. Again the International recommended it would be to the benefit of the employees of the new mill to separate themselves, as it would make for more lucrative contracts. Thus, the second split.

Even with all of this divisiveness, I would not cross our line in 1987, as I could not put myself or mine ahead of my fellow workers.

I also feel that the government is against the working people, and that when it looked like we might win this strike the government, the company and the International Union were against us.

Democratic national candidate Jesse Jackson addressing union rally in Jay, October 12, 1987. Photo by Rene Brochu.

Two Extremes of Feeling in a Second's Time

Gary Labbe

Let me tell you about the most craziest thing that happened on the picket line.

We had super striker nails, the ones that were drilled and tack welded to a washer. We were playing a game on who could position it the best so a scab would pick it up in one of his tires. It was my turn and this scab come through the line. It seemed to me that he was laughing at me and I was so mad that I could of ripped off his head and shit down his throat. The deputy sheriffs was all around watching us to make sure we did not touch their vehicles. Just as he moved forward, the nail found its home—my nail.

So there I was so mad I could see red, then instantly so happy that I got the bastard. Sheriffs all over the place. I wanted to scream with happiness and just a second ago so full of anger. Let me tell you there was *two extremes of feeling in a second's time.*

The Book

Ida Luther

My political career began because of the two paper mill strikes, the Boise strike in Rumford and the International Paper Company strike in Jay.

Francis Perry was the State Representative for District 52, and when he decided to retire, he came to my house on three separate occasions, asking me to run for his seat. Each time my answer was "no thanks."

Then Francis worked on my husband, Charlie, who is a Local 900 member. My husband reasoned with me this way, "If people who care about hourly workers won't run for office, then who will ever hold office that cares about us?" I changed my mind.

I didn't know the first thing about organizing a campaign. Someone advised me to ask a man named Peter Kellman to help me. Charlie and I went to a meeting upstairs at the Local 14 meeting hall in Jay. The meeting was to organize the campaign for Ed Pineau. Local 14 seemed to me then, as it does now, to be always organizing something, and I thank God for that!

We met Peter and he agreed to help, and he did help in so many ways [that] I could write about and fill a book. Mostly, what I remember is he made a calendar for me. For every day from Sept. 1st to election day, there was an instruction of what I should be doing and where I should be doing it. That calendar became my bible. I just did everything as Peter charted it out. I worked my heart out and I won.

I'm happy to be a participant in "The Book" project because I believe in the importance of labor history.

I'm happy to be a participant in "The Book" project because I trust the integrity of Peter Kellman. As long as he doesn't give up on social justice, neither will I.

What the Strike of 1987 Meant to Me

Marie D. Pineau

"THE BIG BOYS PLAYING GAMES WITH MIDDLE AMERICA"

Fight! Resist!

Raymond G. Pineau (Ray from Jay)

The strike of 1987 gave me the opportunity to meet working people from all over the country. It made me realize that I am proud to be in the same category as meat packers, traffic controllers, railroad workers, mine workers, bus drivers, pilots, longshoremen, etc. A number of these people were replaced in the 80s.

We work hard to make corporations and our country prosperous and often-times our efforts are ignored. If corporate management treated us fairly, we would not need unions. However, they have no concept of product, just profit. In our strike, they wanted 13 percent cutback in our wages and benefits and they gave themselves 38 percent wage increases and bonuses.

This disregard for working people reached wherever people worked. It pitted working people against working people using replacement workers, "scabs." A scab is a worker who is willing to sell his skills to the highest bidder even though the pay is less than that of the union worker.

I applaud the workers from Maine who did not cross our picket line, yet were more than skilled enough to replace us. I especially applaud the Maine State Building and Construction Trades who also lost their jobs to BE&K, Cianbro and other scab contractors. I am sorry that I never understood how these people and their families suffered the same indignities as we did as primary mill workers.

If I were to leave a legacy for working people it would be this.

You are the builder, the driver, the painter and butcher, the finisher, etc., and your efforts are what makes this country grand. Your children will feed the hungry, care for the infirm, build the future. You are a tradesperson, either an apprentice, a journeyman or a master. Don't let your skills and efforts go unrewarded. Unite in your trade for better pay, benefits and working conditions. Don't degrade your skill by working for less than your brothers and sisters in your trade. Don't let oppression get you down or go unchecked. *Fight! Resist!*

It is this stubborn refusal to succumb to all odds that joined 13 colonies into one nation.

"IP Unfair," father and son. Photo by Rene Brochu.

My Impressions during 1987 Strike at Androscoggin Mill

Tom Hersey
Class of '87

I think the strike started out as a lark. Surely it would not last long: how long could IP shut down a mill that produced one-fourth of its 1986 profit of 306 million dollars?

For the night shift, of which I was a member, it started at 6:50 A.M. when we were led to the gate. No one asked if we wanted to stay; we were led to the gate as if we had been fired. We had been, but we didn't know it then.

For ten days we stood on the picket line and hassled the company militia (Wackenhut) and any of the imported supervisors from other mills that showed their faces.

One Monday morning ten days after the strike had started, a front page article in the *Sun-Journal* quoted IP's personnel manager K.C. Lavoie as saying that IP would use replacement workers soon, but not right away. That same morning scabs started going through the gate. We had been fired that morning ten days before.

I can't remember everything about the strike, but I can give my impressions of some of the standout events.

My biggest impression is of the weekly meetings. Everyone was invited, including spouses and children. There was a parade of labor leaders, state legislators and college professors. There were national leaders like Representative Gephardt from

Missouri and the Reverend Jesse Jackson. And then there was the visit from Wayne Glenn, president of the International.

Wayne Glenn is a true rebel. He is still fighting the Civil War. He saw his chance to screw some Yankees and he took it. He came here and told us he was behind us 1,000 percent (a 1,000 yards would have been more like it); told us that he couldn't tell us what they used to do to scabs, led us on a march to the mill gates and got the local fined $10,000 for inciting a riot.

My next impression is the influence IP has on state government. Whenever IP had one of its non-events, the DEP never failed to show up one to three days late and/or with the wrong equipment. (A non-event was any incident of pollution ranging from the 16 million gallons of raw sewage spilled into the river to the releasing of a tank car of chlorine in the atmosphere. It was from this latter incident that I got my impression of what IP really thought of the welfare of its workers. Had the wind been blowing the other way they would have been picking bodies off the fence six months later. IP had locked the gates out of fear that the strikers would invade the mill thereby trapping the scabs.)

IP had the governor in its pocket so deep that he began parroting everything that an IP official said. The president of IP was even able to summon him to a meeting in Portland at 2 A.M.

After the strike, the representative to the legislature from this district (a Republican) went to work for IP as the director of communications, and the man who was in charge of water quality for the DEP got a job with IP as their environmental chief.

Even the media had nothing good to say about us. It seemed that everything IP had to say against us, whether true or false, the newspapers or TV printed or put on the air, confirmed or not.

The courts were not much better. Any legal action brought against a striker by IP or one of its scabs was quickly prosecuted, while any charge brought against a scab dragged on and on. And they drag on even to this day.

We did have one friend in the media during the strike, and then he was only a part-time friend. His name is Tom Hanrahan and he worked for Channel 8.

I learned a couple of lessons during the strike. First, I learned that the white American male is the only person on earth that it is still legal to discriminate against, especially if he is over 50. There are no jobs for him.

I also learned how hard it is to buy the "American Dream." It takes two paychecks and even then [a couple] can't afford the upkeep and the "Dream" is falling down around them. If you ask why they don't form unions in an effort to better themselves, you get a lecture on the evils of unionism.

I have been asked to include in this history a letter to the editor that I wrote four years after the strike started. It was quite lengthy so I edited it for publication. I wish I hadn't now.

The first paragraph states how since it's an election year, it's time for our biennial name calling and who is more fiscally responsible, Joe Brennan or Jock McKernan.

The rest of the original letter went like this:

"In 1986, the paper companies began to force upon their workers contracts that called for the elimination of premium time for Sundays and holidays—money that had been offered to the workers to entice them to work those days in the first place. The workers in Rumford struck and 350 of them lost their jobs, despite the moderation efforts of Joe Brennan. In 1987, the same kind of contract was offered the IP workers in Jay. The people in Jay struck and 1,250 lost their jobs, while Jock stood by and did nothing. The same scene was repeated in Bucksport, except that the workers there saw the handwriting on the wall and swallowed the contract. It was either strike and be replaced, or accept. Since then the paper companies have been able to force concessionary contracts on their workers throughout the state.

Now for some math. Every papermaker in the state has lost $5,000 plus per year for four years. (There are 20,000 of them.) It doesn't take a great brain to figure out that this amounts to $400 million. Four hundred million dollars that the state has not collected income nor sales taxes from. A total of $60 million of revenue lost to the state. Nobody knows the cost in failed businesses and lost jobs. How many miles of safe highways and safe bridges or other state services does $60 million buy? How many homes or cars? How many appliances? How many pairs of shoes, dresses, skirts or blouses? How many jobs? How much happiness would the other $340 million buy? All this could have been prevented, but they stood by the side of the paper companies and vetoed strike breaker bills not once, but three times, and the vetoes were upheld three times with the help of Republican legislators."

The person who asked me to include the letter asked that it be included because it turned out to be so prophetic. The state is broke and has had to resort to furloughing workers one day of the month, while services have been cut to the bone and in some cases have even been "privatized."

I suppose I could have broken ranks and crossed the line, but I stayed out. I don't believe in strikes, and I was one of the handful of people that voted against a strike. I believe in unions. I firmly believe that unions have done more for the working man (union and non-union) than all the benevolence of all the employers since time began. That is why I am still a member of a union even though it can no longer represent me. Someday we will, hopefully, have a union back in the mill.

Presidential candidate Dick Gephardt addressing rally at mill gate, November 21, 1987. Photo by Rene Brochu.

The Story Has No End, It's Living History

Maurice Metivier
Local 14 Shop Steward

My name is Maurice Metivier. My wife is Joanne. We have three children, Nicole 17, Kelly 11 and Michael 8. At the time of the strike, Mike was only two months old.

When we left the mill on June 16, I was convinced it was hopeless. It was still brute strength and ignorance (or so I thought) in the wood room where I work.

My wife and I had planned and saved for the strike, so for the first month we went to all the rallies and marches and stayed on the picket line a lot. We were kind of caught up in the excitement and not too concerned about our bills or anything else for that matter.

We were in the middle of building our home so we talked about what we should do and decided to continue on building our home. Finding a job was easy; the pay wasn't very good, but it was an honest living. I worked for Barker Construction as a carpenter. I worked ten-hour days, and nights were divided between teaching CCD (religious ed), picketing, rallies and building our kitchen. We found ourselves getting frustrated; there just wasn't enough money to go round, and we were supplementing my pay by withdrawing money from our savings account. Working on the picket line only added to the frustration—it just seemed so useless.

Six months into the strike I needed an operation on my shoulder, which kept popping out of joint. This had happened at the mill so I was able to collect workers' comp from the mill. This gave me a chance to do something more than picketing, so I started to travel with the caravan. Doing the leafleting and talking to people about corporate greed and our own complacency helped vent my anger. We were in Westbrook at a rally the first time I spoke to a large group of people. From here, I found myself traveling with the caravan. We traveled in Maine, Massachusetts and Rhode Island while I was with it. I spoke in several universities, union halls, grange halls and at some rallies. These people we met really cared about us and supported us. At one rally we were entertained by Yiddish musicians. We stayed at a railroad striker's sister's house. He lost everything he had, but still wanted to help. We also stayed with socialists who were studying us. In Boston, we were put up by a woman and her son in Jamaica Plains. She lived on a meager income, but put my brother-in-law and myself up for two days and gave us five dollars for the cause when we left. We met some terrific people on the caravan. The three months I traveled on the caravan was the most enjoyable and memorable parts of the strike for me. My wife, though she supported our decision to strike, was very angry with me for traveling with the caravan. We would be gone for four or five days at a time and this would really upset her. There were many arguments and fights, but we endured.

My shoulder healed some and IP offered me light duty work at the mill, so I went back pounding nails. Our troubles were just beginning. I got into a bad car accident and totaled our car, and then shortly after replacing it, we lost the transmission. Just when things were beginning to get better, everything went sour again.

In August of '88, my wife started getting sick and two weeks later we were in the middle of hell. Joanne had an aneurysm on her brain and now we found ourselves facing her death. This is when I realized we had an angel watching over us. Joanne's surgery went well and she came out of it normal.

Then, in the course of a week, the union put on a benefit supper for us. Joe Gatts gave us his strike pay. We received a check from someone in Mobile, Alabama, and someone made a house payment for us. This reminded me of the type of people we had gone on strike with, some of the finest people you'd ever want to meet.

Our life was starting to come around, but money was in short supply. The job I had with Barker Construction just wasn't making it for us. I stayed with Barker through the winter, but in early spring me and Mike Cote went into our own business, M & M Builders. This lasted about three months before I ran out of money completely. My wife prompted me to get a job that paid something, so I applied for work at BIW, where I was hired on as a tinsmith. I stayed there for about ten months before I got my letter to return to the mill.

On March 26, I went back to the mill. Our shop steward was still out so I took on the role, and I feel I had the wrong idea of how we should be as union people. I had so much hate in me, it was eating my life up. I was very arrogant and outspoken in the mill, willing to challenge management at the drop of a hat, and treating scabs like the dirt I thought they were. My whole focus was on getting scabs fired so we could get our people back.

The longer I'm in here, the more I realize that's not going to happen. Our people will only come back when the mill decides to bring them back. I've never had anything tear me up inside like this, and here I am one of the lucky ones who got their jobs back. It's taken me three years to stop hating and learn to deal effectively with our situation. Or am I? This becomes another problem in itself, all the uncertainty of anything that happens in here. Some of us feel like traitors because we got our job back. ("We don't go back til we all go back.")

Right now I'm involved in every program that IP has going. I sit in meetings with union, management and scabs, changing the way the workers are handled. There are new systems for moving up instead of by seniority; it's a three-point system: a peer evaluation form, a personnel records check and an interview. I'm working on a design team that forms rules for qualifying and certifying on your current job. I was also sent to New York to Hannaford Brothers Distribution Center, where there is no union but run with the team concept ideas. The concepts I saw there are similar to what they are trying here. I also went to school for a week and learned how to conduct classes in the

DDI concepts. These concepts are Making the Difference, Valu-
ing Differences, Participating in Meetings, Handling Conflict,
Team Start Up, Working in Teams and Communicating with
Others. These concepts are fine, but are what we always used to
work with.

The problem with the concepts are: 1) they are coming from
someone we don't trust, and 2) less than half the people are
back, and they are contesting the rights of 156 of our members.
But I'll tell you my Christian values and my work ethics are
something they will never get me to compromise again. I hope
my actions never hurt anyone. The people of Locals 14 and 246
have been hurt too much already. And to me, it can never be
forgotten that the International sold us out, or just a few leaders
of the International Union. And the last sentence is a crying
shame. It's been eight years now and not a single day has gone
by without a word about the strike. *The story has no end, it's living history.*

I Sat and Cried

Laurier Poulin

At 55 years of age, I did not in my wildest dreams think that I would face unemployment. I had been working as the service inspector for the company for nearly 32 years. I decided to walk off my job because I did not want to give up double time on Sundays and, mostly, I did not want to give up the shut down for Christmas. Christmas to me is a holy holiday to be spent with your families. I believe that Mr. John Georges, CEO of International Paper Company, does spend this day with his family. At least I hope he does.

When I cleaned out my locker on June 15, 1987, and walked out that gate, I had a very heavy feeling in my heart. I thought to myself that I might never work here again and where will I find work at my age. At that time, I still had one son in college. Our other three children were on their own, including one son who walked with the strikers.

My wife was very supportive of the strike. She left her role as a homemaker and went to work at Livermore Falls Shoe on June 19 (her birthday). As she left for work the first morning, I kissed her good-bye, and after the door was closed, I sat and cried. Our beautiful and seemingly tranquil life had been upheaved. Our apple cart was tipped over.

I found work in a school construction site in Hartford. During this time I did my picketing in the evening. After we started getting unemployment, I did picketing duty in the morning so as to be able to see the scabs cross the line. My wife or my college son often picketed with me as a substitute for my striking son who had found employment on Cape Cod in Massachusetts. I also became involved with the food bank. Working there helped me to realize that I was so much better off than a lot of people. Sharing and giving on that food line was a real stimulant for me.

My wife and I attended all the Wednesday night rallies. That was like a booster shot to keep us going for another week. After most of the rallies, my family met in different homes every week and that also helped to keep our morale up.

As a couple, we were on the first caravan on that cold January day. We handed out leaflets in front of K-Mart in Madawaska. When we arrived in our motel room to prepare for dinner, we found our toothpaste, shaving cream and deodorant frozen solid in our suitcases. I went on caravans to New York, Massachusetts, Connecticut, New Jersey, Rhode Island and Delaware. I felt the caravans were doing a good job until the trip to the Bank of Boston was postponed. Then I feel a lot of momentum was lost and we never recovered from that.

My striking son sold his house in Jay in the fall of 1988. The day we emptied his home was another low day during the strike. We both had a very hard time leaving his home for the last time. He very emphatically blamed IP for that sad day.

When the strike was called off on that fateful day in October, I was on the picket line at 6:00 A.M. on that Monday morning. The officer on duty told me that the strike was over, but I did not believe him. Peter Kellman came and got me off the line. I was very upset with the decision to end the strike and felt that we had been sold down the river by the International Union.

After the strike was ended, I found employment at Carlton Woolen in Winthrop until I was called back to work on January 21, 1989. I was the 21st person back and that was a most difficult thing. Only with the help of God did I survive these days. I had a little prayer stuck to the inside of my lunch basket that said, "Lord help me to remember that nothing is going to happen to me today that you and I together cannot handle."

Apparently that prayer helped me, as on May 1, 1994, I have retired from International Paper with very mixed feelings about the company.

We Had to Put Up with These Gestapo Tactics

Maurice Poulin

I am a third-generation worker at the IP mill in Jay, Maine. I am also a striker who lost his job in the strike of 1987. I returned to work in February of 1993.

My maternal grandfather, Joseph Jolicoeur, came down from Canada in the early 1900s to work at the Otis mill in Chisholm, down river from the new IP mill. He retired after about 40 years of service. My father, Arthur Poulin, also worked in the old mill for 42 years. I have three brothers who worked both at the old mill and then at the Androscoggin mill. They are Eugene "Mickey" with 45 years of service, Rene, who worked for the Woodlands department, with 36 years and Laurier with 40 years of service. I now have, in 1994, 39 years with the company. I also have an uncle, Andrea Jolicoeur, with 45 years of service and his son, Gerard Jolicoeur, with 38 years of service. Also there are two nephews, Daniel Poulin with 27 years, and Jim Cieslak with 27 years. The total years that my family has given in service to the ungodly IP comes to a grand total of 379 years.

I am emphasizing this great number of faithful service to show that it is unbelievable that a company would forget all of this service and dedication of lifetimes and, in 1987, would replace all of us with one swipe of their greedy corporate hand. How heartless, how cruel can a company be? It is almost like we had our own holocaust at the hands of the IP thugs. I can

51

now see how Hitler destroyed millions of Jews and got away with it for so long. The IP did the same to us and destroyed hundreds of lives, livelihoods, families and, yes, even causing several of us to have stress-related heart attacks, some of them being fatal.

I had my heart attack in December of 1988, just a couple of months after the UPIU abandoned us on that fateful October 10, 1988, a date that will go down in infamy and be remembered for generations to come. I was lucky and miraculously was brought back to life, thanks to the excellent emergency services in our town of Jay. I was out of work for three months recuperating at home. By then I had a job in another paper mill and was traveling 60 miles a day, six days a week.

During the strike, my lovely wife was working all the overtime that she could at a local nursing home. Her financial help prevented us from going into debt. Also we had the food bank and the moral support of our family and other strikers.

How do I feel about the strike? I am angry that the mighty IP did this to us. They stole our jobs and gave them to scabs. I am angry that the International Union let us sink with the ship. I am bitter and sad that in a free country *we had to put up with these Gestapo tactics.*

I am now back to work at the IP, but I don't have my previous job yet and I am making less money. A scab still has my position and I will retire before I replace the scab.

Outside of the mill, I have learned to live with what we had to endure. My future pension will be cut down by almost $200 a month because our time out of the mill does not count as time worked.

I am happy and joyful when I am with my family, children, grandchildren and friends. My faith in God and my Catholic religion sustain me.

The IP now say after seven years that all is behind us. I cannot truthfully put the hideous actions of the company behind me, no more than I can tell the sun not to rise tomorrow.

My father was on strike in 1921. He never regained real financial security. He told all of us boys to never go on strike. "It does not pay," he said. God rest his soul, he was right.

How about the future of my children and grandchildren?

Well, a sister-in-law and my son's aunt, who sided with IP during and since the strike, told my son at a bitter family reunion, "This strike is generational, and it will go with this generation." My wise son replied, "This strike will last forever; my children will not forget what the IP did to my father, and to all the other union people." He is right.

As I began this testimony, I mentioned that I was the third generation to work at the IP in Jay, and I believe that it will be at least another three generations before the hurt and the pain of the strike of 1987 is even begun to be forgotten or forgiven.

This Will Never Heal

Mike Hartford

June 1987 was the happiest time in my life. My son Brandon was born at 12:14 P.M. Several hours later I was on strike. As my new family and I sat on the hospital bed, I watched family and friends man the picket lines on the television set. The next day, I had a job working construction for half the money I was making at the mill. This job lasted six months. Two days before Christmas I was laid off. Money was very tight as we had just bought the house. I worked enough overtime to cover the bills, and the strike fund was paying for the food. The new baby was allergic to milk, so he was on special formula and with his diapers and other essentials I figured Rhonda, my wife, was feeding us for about $35 a week. We ate a lot of noodles and spaghetti sauce and peanut butter and jelly sandwiches. The food bank provided us with the essential groceries.

Soon after Christmas, our car died. The motor was blown and we didn't have the money for a motor. The car sat in the driveway all winter. Come summer, the car was sold for parts. My wife was home alone with no vehicle and a sick toddler. After Christmas, I got a job as a plumber's helper in Gorham, Maine. The pay covered the bills, so I moved my wife and my six-month old son into my parents' home so that we could be together. This was very trying for my wife and myself. We fought constantly. We stayed for eight months. Then, we moved back to Wilton. I traveled 150 miles a day, leaving at 5:00 A.M. and never knowing when I would get home. The days were long for

Rhonda since she had no car and had to do all of the work that I should have been doing. Thank God that she didn't complain much.

On Fridays, this was my salvation. We manned the picket lines, screaming at the scabs. Going against how I wanted my son to treat people, but this cause was right and sometimes you have to go against your values to achieve the right goal.

The day the strike was called off, I was working in Biddeford. My heart sank when I heard the news. Sixteen months of back-breaking, low-paying jobs, family separation, all for nothing because nine men could out-vote the 4,000 plus union men and women who fought and refused to give up. We fought long and hard for what we believed in, but I guess it didn't matter. I may never know why these men called off the strike and, if I do, it will never change my mind. If they worried about people crossing the picket lines and being super scabs, then they should not have been in that position because we all lost our solidarity and our livelihood forever. This fight was to have IP treat everyone equally. If the company made money, then everyone should make money, not just the CEOs. We wanted good wages and benefits and, most of all, to be treated as proud men and women, not numbers.

The strike ended eight years ago. I work at Boise Cascade now. Times have changed. I now have two boys and a better life. I took my buyout in 1993, and will never return. They say that time heals all wounds, but they are wrong. *This will never heal.* As I drive past the old International Paper Company mill, the hate creeps up. They have ruined families economically and personally. They have ruined the town of Jay and families.

If the people in the unions do not come together and actively participate in the union, this may happen again. We must educate the people and our kids, for they are the future. If not, the future only holds scabs taking our jobs.

Last, but not least, I must thank my wife Rhonda of 11 years for standing by me through the strike, and my son Brandon, who I couldn't spend much time with because I was working all the time. My youngest son, Jacob, was born after the strike. He has no understanding about the strike and I hope through his lifetime he never will. I feel sorry for the families who did not make it through the tough times of the strike.

On the Picket Line Again

Joe Salatino

Joe graduated from high school in 1970. He worked at Laverdieres Drug Store in Rumford until he got hired in the Boise mill in 1983, where he worked in various jobs until he won a bid in the Goundwood mill.

In the spring of 1986, Local 900 struck Boise and Joe was out on the picket line. He figured he'd be out for a couple of weeks and that would be that. He heard that Boise was going to bring scabs, and so he called the hall. Don Barker said that he didn't think that Boise would replace the strikers. Wrong! Then he got a call telling him if he didn't come back, he would be replaced.

He picketed and looked for work, and finally found work as a mason in Bath. He received a call from his wife saying that IP company wanted to hire him in the fall of 1986, and so he went to work in Jay. He warned the IP workers when they were talking strike that they would probably be replaced. On June 16, 1987, Local 14 struck IP. Even before the strike, IP had brought in trailers for the scabs.

Joe found himself *on the picket line again.* He was called back to work for a maintenance job in the fall of 1987.

Joe said that only a lowlife would cross a picket line and he never considered this an option in the Jay strike. Some of the people that hired in with Joe crossed the line in Jay. Joe, being one of four generations of papermakers, who had worked in the Rumford plant, understood full well what being union was.

His only comment was that "it is too bad a company has to treat its people that way."

Here We Go Again

Jim Bartash

At the time of the interview, Jim was working for Boise Cascade Corporation in Rumford, Maine.

Jim started his career in the paper industry after graduating from high school in 1966 for Oxford Paper Company in Rumford. Subsequently, Oxford was sold to Ethyl Corporation, which sold much of the previous mill off for quick profit, and then sold again to Boise Cascade Corporation. Boise started putting money into the mill in upgrades, including #15 paper machine in 1980. In 1986, Boise wanted concessions in premium pay, holidays and work rules. Local 900 UPIU struck in June. Jim felt that the strike would not last too long, that it was not "a big deal." There wasn't any warning of being replaced. Boise brought in scabs and still most of the workers were not worried. Jim said they really became concerned when they were replaced. Jim didn't look for work immediately and picketed night times and weekends, as some of his fellow strikers were working elsewhere. At this time, Jim still wasn't worried; the scabs were placed on easy-to-operate equipment, like computerized #15 machine, etc., as there was no time to train them.

In September of 1986, Jim was hired at IP. He almost missed the call as no one was home . . . initially. Others [who were] called refused, and so Jim received another call and agreed to work for IP. He told the IP guys about being replaced and they said that there was no way that IP would replace them. He showed them a 20-year anniversary knife that he received from Boise, with a note saying that they hoped there were no hard feelings.

In June of 1987, Local 14 UPIU struck IP. *Here we go again*: when asked why he didn't cross this line, Jim said that this was not an option to be considered for you don't do that to the people you work with. This strike brought unity to the labor movement and it was felt that we had a chance to win.

In the fall of 1987, Jim was recalled to Boise, and he harbored much anger toward the scabs; one scab would do some of Jim's work and he would make a point of not thanking this individual.

Jim struck two companies and was replaced twice in a year by scabs. He has kept an outstanding loyalty to the unions and feels that the times were the cause of these conflicts.

The Foremen Talk

Thomas Hersey

The date was January 2nd, 1992, and I had just put my daughter and her husband on the plane back to North Dakota. Instead of going straight home, I decided to stop off at the union hall to see what was up. As I walked through the door, someone said that Felix Jacques wanted to see me. I went in to see him and he told me to pack my lunch, that I was going to work 3 to 11. I asked if this was a joke and he said no. I then told him that I wasn't going in then, but I would go in the next Monday. Felix picked up the phone and called the mill and told them that I would be in Monday morning. Then I knew for sure that it was no joke.

Monday morning I went in for my physical and it wasn't long before a scab came in and wanted to know where the nearest unemployment office was. (I was going back on the very day that the company was laying off because of lack of orders.) I told him that it would be in Rumford and he asked "how do I get there?" I gave him directions and asked where he was from. "Kingfield," he replied. I thought to myself that there was a guy who could find his way to Jay to scab a job, but couldn't find his way to Rumford to get unemployment compensation. About then the nurse came back and introduced us to each other, mentioning that I was coming back. It took about a minute for the light to come on and the look on his face said it all. I am getting laid off and the company is calling back one of the strikers—what in hell is going on?

While I was still taking my physical, one of the scabs that had been brought up from the South (you know, those southern Maine counties of Alabama, Louisiana and Texas) came for something to put on his hands, the palms of which were raw. When he was asked how he had done that, he replied that he had been chipping ice from his driveway. I told him that he could wait and the ice would melt. I thought to myself that these people, by what I had seen so far, were not too smart. Anyway, my physical was over and Dave Walters had come to pick me up and tell me that I was assigned to 4 & 5 converting until the layoffs were over.

Two weeks later, I went back to the same department that I had been in when we went out, only now instead of a stack helper, I was a trainee and working with the computer was my job. It didn't take long to find out that scabs ran the mill. One of the first crew meetings I attended, a scab from stock prep called the paper machine supervisor stupid for not using a chemical that he preferred over a chemical that they were using at the time. Another scab told this same supervisor that he realized that he (the supervisor) was still wet behind the ears, but how did he think that the people on the supers were going to operate if they had to use the ice shack [small, windowed, air-conditioned structures in middle of the huge, very hot paper machine rooms used for workers to cool off] out of the machine to get cooled off. The supervisor got red in the face, but he sat there and took it. It appeared he had no choice.

Of course, I got my chance to find out what kind of people I was working with my first day in my own department. All I had to do was go to the toilet. The sink had a hunk taken out of it, the urinal had a couple of hunks taken out of it and even the flush had a hunk taken out of it. Even in the super room itself, if something was dropped, it laid where it landed. If it was in the way, it was kicked to one side. The stacks and winder had oil and dust on them half an inch thick. They were never wiped down because, if the paper machine went down, the people on the supers were sent to the machine to help get it going.

Something that took a while for me to become aware of was

the fact that the foremen talked only to scabs. They would walk past a striker to ask a scab how things were running. One of them walked by me one day and asked a scab from #3 salvage winder how #2 winder was running and how the paper was coming out.

It took about two months for me to have my first run-in with not one, but two, scabs all at the same time. It was just before 7:00 A.M. and we were cutting a Japanese order when the operator came and asked me not to send any paper downstairs. (He was concerned about the production.) The second helper came and told me to send paper downstairs. The operator came back and asked why I was sending paper downstairs. The operator and helper argued between themselves until I had all I could take and blew up. I was not going to be pushed and pulled around like a puppet.

"Okay," I said, "let's make up your (expletive deleted) minds about what we're going to do!" Some say I was heard all the way to the machines when I let go. Anyway, we compromised and sent paper downstairs. I commented to a foreman, who came by later, that IP was going to get what it deserved. The teams they created were competing to see how much paper they could ship and all manner of crap was going out the door. He kept his silence and I took that to mean, "no comment."

Well, it is four years later. These are some of the things that have stuck in my mind. Not much has changed. The operator and the helper still argue between themselves. If something is dropped, it stays where it fell. There have been some changes though. I am not asked to hold paper until the hour. We have our own ice shack. The scabs say they aren't babied even though the company put in a cafeteria for them. (It's the only one throughout the company.) And we get a raise every time the scabs vote to keep the union out.

I Stand as Solid as Ever

Phyllis J. Luce

I went to work in the International Paper Company in 1984. After standing in long lines to apply for a job year after year, I was finally hired for summer help. After working that first summer, I was asked to stay on along with 14 others who had come to work at the same time.

I was divorced in 1983 and still had a 15-year-old to support on my own. This job was my salvation, this job was my security, this job was going to help me get through anything that came up.

In 1987, the big strike came. I was devastated by the actions. Families turning against families. Sisters and brothers of union people crossing the lines and both being bashed by one another. We fought long and hard to hold onto our solidarity and the UPIU members made extraordinary efforts to hold us all together and fight for our rights, but without any ground. The strike has left a lot of bad memories and a lot of relatives not speaking. As far as I'm concerned, we cannot hold a grudge forever. It's not the union workers or the replacements, but the giant corporations who caused all the trouble and loved every minute of it. I went to work in places at minimum wage after the strike. My daughter and I ate a lot of peanut butter sandwiches and a lot of bologna, but I held my ground for what I believed in. Nothing is solved. Nobody won! Life goes on, but what our forefathers

I only hope the new generation can learn from us that, no matter what we lose or gain, we should always hold on to what we believe in and stand solid on the ground and not be pushed into anything for money, because we all have a conscience and it will catch up with us in the future.

I stand as solid as ever in solidarity, even though things have changed and nothing makes sense to the working people. We can't live in this world and work without unions, so we must always think of this and be active in whatever is going on in your town and community. And vote for who you believe in.

1988 National Democratic Convention, Atlanta, Georgia. Photo by Judith Glickman.

Jay, Maine, Lauded

(Letter to the Editor written during the strike)

Joni Piney

Letter to the Editor:

I am a Local 1787 union member currently on strike at the International Paper Company, Lock Haven, Pennsylvania, plant. I am proud to belong to a union not afraid to fight for our rights. We, the people of the United States of America, have got to get involved in this battle now! If we sit back and let the large corporations do what they want to do, our children will suffer dearly.

I was recently part of a group that attended a statewide rally in Jay, Maine. The rally was for the people that were on strike at the IP plant located there. The support these people have is overwhelming. The town fire company led the march, blowing their horns to let IP know we were there.

Of course, when they saw 8,700 people marching on their plant, I'm sure they realized what a battle we are going to give them. At the rally, the town police were walking around talking to everyone. I walked up to one of the policeman and said, "This is great. We do not have this kind of support in Lock Haven." His reply was, "We live in this town too." I could be wrong, but I don't believe there is a union in Maine that wasn't represented at this march. Also, the state politicians were not afraid to come out and speak for the rights of the working man.

We could not have asked for a better reception than we received in the town of Jay, Maine. When we told these people we are from Lock Haven, Pennsylvania, there wasn't enough they could do for us. We were taken into their homes and treated better than family. When I expressed my doubts about the future, I was told, "Don't worry. We will win this battle for you right here in Jay, Maine." I returned to Lock Haven with high spirits and feeling confident. As long as we have brothers and sisters like this, we will win. Many thanks to the people of Jay for the hospitality and support we received.

We are currently planning a statewide rally to be held in Lock Haven. We are aiming for a date of August 22nd. We need 100 percent support from our small city. We will have people coming from Jay, Maine, Mobile, Alabama, plus all the people from our state and surrounding states. I plead with everyone to open your homes and hearts to these people. We are all in this together.

We must take a stand now for the working man of America. We must not let greed blind us, as it has done to the rich. We are the backbone of this country. We are the working people making the products that make these people rich. We realize we will never come close to the rich people's standard of living. We just want to be comfortable. What is wrong with that?

One question to the people crossing the picket line and taking our jobs: Do you realize, we are fighting for your future and your children's future?

"Help, Stop," march and rally in Lock Haven, Pennsylvania, August 22, 1987.

Stood Firm Her Ground

F.C. (Bud) Budinger and Family
August 24, 1987

Dear Brothers and Sisters:

A very special THANK YOU to Local 14 and especially to all who came to Lock Haven to support our August 22nd labor march and rally.

Merely saying thank you somehow seems to be so inadequate for the enormous amount of personal gratitude I personally feel for you, my brothers and sisters from Jay, Maine. I have been a UPIU member for 22 years. I have been involved in three strikes during my employment at Hammermill-International Paper companies, this current strike being the third. During the first two strikes, one in 1968 and the second in 1972, I personally felt more like a leper than a striker, as did many of the strikers at this paper mill. Unfortunately, here in Lock Haven we do not have the community support as you have in your area. Over the years, even other unions in the Hammermill Council chose to let us fight our battles here in Lock Haven with the company on our own. Many times, not only did we find our local union out on the limb alone, other Hammermill unions held the ladder while the company sawed off the limb. Needless to say, Local 1787 stood alone for a good many years, BUT NO MORE!

Words can never express my heartfelt appreciation for the

out-pouring of emotional and physical support you people have given me and my union brothers and sisters here in Lock Haven. It is truly God's blessing that a bridge of friendship and solidarity has emerged to span the miles between Jay, Maine, and Lock Haven, Pennsylvania. For the first time in 22 years, as a union member I know the true meaning of the words united, comrade and solidarity.

In order that some of you who came to Lock Haven for the rally might know who is writing this letter, I am the brother who was in charge of the transportation/taxi service for the march and rally on August 22nd. Some of you might remember me as the union brother who boarded your bus when it was stopped at the railroad crossing when you first arrived in Lock Haven. I am a proud union member for many reasons. Not only am I proud of what this union stands for, I am proud to tell you that Ron Shearer, officer and spokesman for our local, is my son. I also have the proud distinction of being the father of a spunky young, handicapped daughter—an IP company employee—who *stood firm her ground* and refused to cross our picket line to work for the company during the strike, even though she knew it could cost her job.

I regret that I was so busy organizing the transportation operations, [that] I did not have the opportunity of meeting and getting to know more of you who came to Lock Haven this past weekend. I hope to remedy that, as my wife, daughter and myself will be stopping by to say hello and deliver a hat to one of our brothers, Bill Harlow, sometime around the first of September.

Again, please accept my deep gratitude for your generous and touching gestures of friendship and support. My family and I shall never forget what you people have done to lift our spirits and our morals here in Lock Haven. God bless and protect you all.

Your Lock Haven Brother, in Solidarity—

An Open Letter to Peter Kellman, "88"

Anonymous

Peter Kellman: This letter is addressed to all those involved in the effort to stop corporate greed.

On the numerous Wednesday night meetings and on the rally get together, you along with other union leaders and supporters have all said the same statement to the 1,200 union members in Jay, who remain on strike:

UNITED YOU STAND — DIVIDED YOU FALL

Well Mr. Kellman, IP understands those same words. That's why back in the mid-to-late-'70s, former IP president, J. Stanford Smith, said, and I quote: "By 1987 there will be no unions at IP." This statement was made after IP split up the bargaining contract unit down to individual mill contracts. By doing this, unions didn't stand together any longer, and thus began to fall to a point where we are today.

In the beginning of this ordeal, the 1,200 membership of Local #14 and #246 (IBFO—International Brotherhood of Firemen and Oilers) . . . were encouraged to take a strike vote to help the troubled Mobile [Alabama] membership. We hopped on the bandwagon to unite our union membership, as it once was. Since we joined in, there was a chance to unite several memberships to join and gather strength to the "fight corporate greed" effort.

This crusade to fight corporate greed could have had the strength it needed if:

- laws pertaining to replacement workers were changed to favor unions and not management.
- big business didn't own the NLRB.
- supervisory personal would have said enough is enough and backed their former employees.
- most importantly, the support of other IP union memberships at the other mills whose contracts came about since we took the stand. If even one or two mills at Corinth, Pine Bluff, Moss Point or the mill in Oregon would have joined the crusade, it would have thinned out management into a divided position where they could not possibly run those plants, especially now that we are headed into the cold weather of winter. It could have sent IP to the bargaining table to negotiate rationally instead of what they did.

IP won't defeat us, we are our own worst enemy. IP is laughing at our own inability to organize our own memberships at these other locations. They are the true members of a union's effort to control corporate greed. The blame should be put on the national leadership. How come Wayne Glenn hasn't reappeared in Jay to encourage our efforts and raise morale during these hard times? [What about] the leadership at those other IP plants for not insisting that their memberships join in and become united—as we were in the '70s, a strong force to control corporate takeover?

If we could have picked up some of those other mills, we wouldn't have had to turn to Ray Rogers as a method of last resort. United we stand, divided we fall doesn't mean one union location; it means all memberships at all locations. All the locals, on strike or locked out, are the true union leaders fighting to stop what is yet to come if we do not unite. I hope and pray that this is not the beginning of the end for unions and middle-class America.

Mr. Meserve once said, "There is no economic justification for these concessions." Truer words were never spoken. How true, when IP clearly refused any contract extension offer. Can the National take IP to court and sue them for the employees jobs back, back wages and the emotional stress they put on the union members and their families?

United We Stand

Peter Kellman

Two press releases I wrote, one before the strike started and one after the strike ended, encompass most of what the struggle means to me.

Press release of June 4, 1987: UNITED WE STAND

PATCO stood alone and we watched, Rumford stood alone and we watched, Bucksport stood alone and we watched. Today we voted to stand united with four other mills. If we go down, IP goes down. By a vote of 98 percent, UPIU Local 14 and IBFO [International Brotherhood of Firemen and Oilers] Local 246 voted to strike IP. We are pooling our votes with locals in Wisconsin, Mississippi, Alabama and Pennsylvania. If International Paper won't bargain in good faith with us, we will all go out.

Next time, Bucksport and Rumford will not stand alone. We will not allow a greedy corporation to wreck our community. If they make a fair profit, and they have, they must pay fair wages. If they make a fair profit, and they have, they must pay their fair share of taxes, and they haven't.

We stand united in support of legislation to require paper companies to replant what they cut. We oppose the dumping of hazardous waste.

A strike vote today is a vote in the future of this state and her people. We don't want to leave our children a world they can't earn a living in, a world with no future.

Labor has always wanted more—more education, better air, cleaner water and, most of all, dignity.

(Sixteen months later)
Press release of October 10, 1988: BUT THE WAR CONTINUES

The strike which began on June 16, 1987 in Jay, Maine, has come to an end. The war being waged by corporate America against workers continues. Workers in Jay, Maine, Lock Haven, Pennsylvania, and De Pere, Wisconsin, announced today that we are ending our strike against International Paper, but will continue to defend ourselves and fight for justice by every means at our disposal.

This stage of the war is over. In a time of record profits, International Paper will get massive concessions from workers who made IP the largest paper company in the world.

We have lost this battle, but the war for justice in the workplace is not over. This battle has touched the lives of millions of workers and the flame of freedom burns as brightly in American workers as it does in Polish workers.

We are proud of the stand we took. Wherever we go, whatever we do, we will continue this fight.

Whatever it takes, for as long as it takes.

We All Need to Stick Together

Mike Cavanaugh, Amalgamated Clothing &
Textile Workers Union

The strike in Jay in 1987-88 is, of course, an event that touched me and members of our union. The year 1987 had already been great trouble for us, as 1,000 workers from the Health Tex plants lost their jobs when the corporation pulled out of Maine in March of '87. Up close and personal, we were facing a corporate culture that easily disposed of workers and hurt their communities severely.

The clothing workers in our union, who had recently become victims of corporate greed themselves, were feeling mixed emotions about Jay. "At least they have jobs" was a common refrain. But when we arrived in Jay on a Saturday for a huge march and rally, a number of our unemployed members understood how much they had in common with the striking paper workers of Jay. *"We all need to stick together"* was the watchword.

Again and again, as we returned to Jay for marches, Wednesday night meetings and picket line help, I was always struck by the sense of community we all shared. The common struggle helped to define the sense of community—that we're all in this together.

For me, the personal issue was how to build common bond between the (relatively) well-paid paper workers and the low-wage production workers of the clothing plants and textile mills. We had some successes, but so did our opposition. Destroying our common bond as working people was a main goal of theirs. Building our solidarity across lines of race, sex, education level and nationality is our challenge for the future. Our failure to do so would be the greatest tragedy of Jay; our commitment to do so will be our most important victory.

"Scabs Out, Union In," march to the mill, November 21, 1987. Photo by Ed Slick.

Scabs Out, Union In

Vinny O'Malley

I have my memories of the strike in Jay—mass meetings, marches on the gates, leaflets and picketing, and solidarity with the membership of Local #14. I'm not sure I could point out any particular event, except possibly the mass march to the mill the day on November 8 when I saw Congressman Dick Gephardt was in attendance. I was up near the entrance when the scabs unfolded the Confederate flag on the roof. I do not think that if I was a Local #14 member that I could have shown the restraint that they did. Obviously, my first reaction was knock the goddamn gate down and take that piece of crap down. But cooler heads prevailed, including Congressman Dick Gephardt. The flag was taken down and the scabs were removed from view.

I have been in plenty of demonstrations that had many more people in attendance, but I will say the feeling I got being part of this mass of union people was one I will never forget. I think I was hoarse for two weeks from yelling, *"Scabs Out, Union In."* I have been truly blessed to meet and befriend so many heroes of workers. God bless and keep them.

In Solidarity—

It Gave Me New Hope for Our Country

Mitch Goodman

Those big meetings at the community building in Jay: I was bowled over—and yes, at times the tears came into my eyes. I hadn't seen this kind of warmth, the heat! I'd never seen anything like it. And that it should be happening during the years of absolute selfishness of the Reagan-Bush era, I could hardly believe it. Here were people coming together for the sake of their union, their community, to meet head on the assault of one of the world's biggest corporations. These were people who had been listless, half-asleep, willing to trust an employer they had known for most of their lives, but now [that] they knew the real nature of IP, they were awake. They were turning to one another again, as I had seen people do . . . growing up in the Great Depression, and millions of Americans woke up.

I came to the meetings as a supporter of the strike, someone who has always believed in unions and worked with them, because I knew that in the dog-eat-dog world we live in (dominated by the big dogs of the corporations and their lackeys in Washington), workers needed one another. Everywhere you went you heard the same story: There is no real working class left, everyone has fallen for the middle-class crap, all they want is to be good consumers. Well, there in Jay I saw how wrong the story was. *It gave me new hope for our country* at a time when so many Americans had fallen for the Reagan line.

The action of the IP workers reminded me of one of the most

important moments of my boyhood. It was 1935-36 and the CIO was being organized. It was happening from the bottom up, as with the Steelworkers Organizing Committee, real rank-and file-action. The same was happening among the auto workers, the textile workers, the rubber workers and others. (For an accurate and exciting history of that time, read Jeremy Brecher's book, *Strike!* [Boston: South End Press, 1972]. It tells the story of why real rank-and-file democracy is the key to strong unions, and why undemocratic top-down bureaucracy in the international unions has killed their spirit.) To be at those meetings in Jay, to hear people speaking for themselves and ready to help one another in real democratic ways, was like a return to those great days of the CIO. [The days] when Americans turned away from the bread-and-butter unionism of a dog-eat-dog society, turning back to one another and realizing that there was more to life then fancy cars and boats and big TVs. Realizing, in fact, that their lives depended on one another—just as their fathers and grandfathers had done in the Great Depression.

The corporations (and their lackeys in Washington and the state capitals) would like us to believe that unions are a thing of the past. A union, unlike a corporation, is a human organism, a fact of life, rooted in real human values: loyalty, equality, compassion. A corporation is a financial mechanism that makes use of people and throws them away. In a union, there is strength and decency—and the best hope for a more humane society.

I Did Not Walk Out Those Doors Alone

Debra H. and Kenneth D. Timberlake

I am the daughter of a man who dedicated the major part of his life to the pulp mill of IP Company. I was raised to believe that this company was special, so when the phone call came in April of 1978 telling me I would be hired in the main lab, I was thrilled. I gave a week's notice at the school where I was employed as a teacher assistant.

I really enjoyed my job and meeting the people. It seemed like one big happy family where people all worked together.

Then the big day came. I reported to work for 6 A.M. to clean my locker rooms and offices. At 7 A.M. I walked out the front doors of IP for the last time. It was a gorgeous summer day and I never dreamed I would never go back to IP Company. At the most, I would have the summer off. BE&K were all there watching with all their trailers lined up.

I did not walk out those doors alone that day. My husband also worked at IP, hired in September of 1977. We got married and had three children, all while working at IP.

We both worked hard on the picket lines. I volunteered time manning the phones in the union hall. We went to the mass meetings as often as possible. We witnessed apologies from people who had crossed the lines and come back out; a man announcing his intent to cross the lines; solidarity of hundreds of union families, holding hands and singing together; my mother working the lines of the food bank (the wife of a salaried employee); and much more.

My husband went through many jobs before finally getting a job at S.D. Warren in Skowhegan in 1991. I was lucky to get a job in MSAD [Maine School Administrative District] #36 in September of 1987. I am now a second grade teacher and very happy.

We are happy with our decision, to fight for what we believe in. There are happy memories along with sad memories. It is one experience in my life that will be with me forever.

Local 14 union band at a mass meeting. Photo by Rene Brochu.

We Will Never Forget

Interview with Arthur Raymond

I went to work for International Paper Company during World War II, somewhere around V.E. Day. I immediately joined the union as my father was, and had always been, a strong union man. He struck IP in 1921, and never returned to work until 1936.

He told me that during that strike, super scabs were made bosses. My father always said that you need violence to stop the scabs. The scabs in 1921 came in boxcars and kicked the daylights out of the townspeople, until the townspeople started rising up and kicking the scabs.

Then the laws were passed to decrease the violence by handcuffing the unions. I told my father that I didn't think IP would do this again. I told Dad that he was wrong, times had changed. But, in the end he was right.

Boy, was he right, boxcars full of scabs in 1921, and trailers full of scabs in 1987! When they brought in the scabs, crack cocaine in massive amounts started showing up everywhere in the area. I talked to an off-duty Auburn detective recently who told me this:

"My father and I went to the store when he was 77 years old, and he was approached by another older man who said hello. My father said, 'Hi, scab. *We will never forget.'*"

The big thing for me in our strike in 1987 was the hurt [to] the people in the community. Friends couldn't make ends meet, divorces, deaths, etc. You could see the pain in their faces.

[Arthur retired from Bath Iron Works in 1995 on the 28th of April, never having returned to IP. He was active in his ship-builders union, keeping an eye out for non-union contractors.]

Really Made Me Feel Good

Interview with Bob Roy

Q: How did you participate during the strike?

A: Oh, the picket line a while until I got kicked off.

Q: Why did you get kicked off?

A: Oh, their doors seemed to open when they went by me. After that, I was a rover.

Q: What is a rover?

A: A rover goes from picket gate to picket gate checking on the status of the picketers. My shift was usually from 7 to 11 at night.

Q: You still called that picket duty?

A: Yes, sometimes three or four times a week during the strike.

Q: Would you bring something to the picketers?

A: Sometimes coffee and donuts or whatever people would bring in for the picketers.

Q: How many gates were there?

A: Wood gate, crash road, the main gate and the Riley gate. (That was a railroad gate.)

Q: How often would you go around?

A: Once every hour.

Q: Did you get involved with setting up the ice shacks for the winter picketing?

A: No, they were already set up by the members who donated them.

Q: Did you also bring wood around?

A: Yes, as we had some wood cut up at the union hall.

Q: Did you start getting active right off on June 16th?

A: Immediately on the morning of June 16th.

Q: How long before you went to work?

A: I worked part-time jobs initially and collected unemployment for about two months.

Q: Did you have to go to Mountain Valley Training for Dislocated Workers to collect your unemployment?

A: Yes, I went to that in Farmington and Wilton.

Q: Did you go to East Millinocket to work on their #6 paper machine rebuild, as many strikers did in the summer of '87?

A: Yes, I went up for a couple of weeks and worked as a carpenter for the Bangor local.

Q: Did it upset you to see the scabs go through the line?

A: Yes, a little bit. I even tried to make them go around.

Q: Should Local 14 have used more violence?

A: First day, yes, but that is the only time. I don't think the strike would have lasted if we had thrown some scabs into the river.

Q: Wouldn't the government have stepped in?

A: Yes, the National Guard would have been called in, but I didn't care.

Q: What was the most [important] moment of the strike as you remember?

A: One night, Jim Lyman and I were roving and we were at one of the gates—no, it was when we got back to the hall— [when] someone gave us a check from their local to our locals. They were from out of town and the check was for a good amount. They wanted to know what to do with it. This happened on a Wednesday night and the mass meeting was going on. I had never been to one, as I did picket duty on that night because picketers were hard to find on meeting night. We went to the gym and brought the check to Bill, who was in the middle of his presentation. I walked across the floor and handed him the check, told him where it came from and he told the crowd. They broke into thunderous applause and I will never forget how it choked me up and *really made me feel good.*

Stand Up for Labor

Interview with Bernard "Nookie" Boivin

Upon graduation from Jay High School in 1958, Nookie started work at Livermore Falls Shoeshop. He worked there until September 16th, 1960, when he was called in to work at the Otis mill. Even though the pay was better at Livermore Shoe, he opted for Otis because of the union environment. His father and brothers worked at Otis mill and told him of the stability of a union contract. Nookie joined Local 14 and remained on the spare list for seven years until a permanent position opened up. Nookie was with Local 14 and IP until he was disabled, January 8th, 1987.

Local 14 struck in June of 1987 and he was terminated by the company during the strike because of his disability. When he started receiving social security because of his disability, IP had to give him his pension.

On June 16th, 1987, Nookie became very active in helping Local 14 win the strike. That is the time when he first became active. Prior to that, Nookie said he was complacent and felt that everything would take care of itself and we didn't have to worry. Prior to the strike, he hadn't even registered to vote.

All of that changed drastically with the strike. He became involved immediately with the creation of the job bank that helped place strikers in various employments throughout the state during the strike. He coordinated with state unemployment commission to help strikers meet criteria to receive unemployment benefits. He helped organize a coalition of building trade unions with in-plant locals to pressure non-union contractors like BE&K, Cianbro, Bancroft and others, who were taking union jobs and turning them into scab jobs and undermining wages and benefits.

Nookie and his wife, Phyllis, were also unofficial human services coordinators for the strikers, helping with every conceivable problem striker families encountered, from suicide to substance abuse and job training, 24 hours a day, seven days a week throughout the strike. He was a liaison between strikers and the solution to some of their problems.

At the end of the strike, he became involved with the political process, especially trying to get union brothers elected to all kinds of offices. He is an active member of the Jay town Democrats and the Franklin county Democrats.

"You have to stand up for labor. With the unions you have agreements, without the unions you have nothing but idle promises. I didn't fear big business, as I figured they would take care of me. I didn't think that they would try to bust the union. We needed the other mills on board to win the strike. Young people need a good education. When I started, six guys applied for one job, now 25 apply for maybe one job."

Like the Rat He Is

Interview with John (Tex) Wilson
(conducted by Ray Pineau and Peter Kellman)

I was in Rumford with my wife on February 5th, 1988, when we heard of a gas leak in Jay that required evacuation of parts of the town, including the school system. When we drove into Jay, we tried to locate our granddaughter. There was much panic and parents all over town were trying to locate their children. We finally located our granddaughter in Wilton.

Later that afternoon, Tex went to the union hall to find out what caused the leak. Scabs had broken a pipe in the pulp mill at IP and thousands of gallons of chlorine dioxide escaped into the community. From the union hall, everyone went to the town office, as Charlie Noonan, the town manager, wanted the mill closed down, but Governor John McKernan was coming. The governor acted like a company stooge and said the mill would not be shut down.

Then it happened. Tex, who was outside of the town office, was used as a diversion to get the governor out of Jay. A state trooper by the name of Red Therrien pushed Tex down over a 15-foot embankment, and when everyone came to see what was going on, the governor was scurried out of Jay *like the rat he is.*

The next day, Tex couldn't walk and had to go to the hospital. At the time, Tex was 54 years old, disabled and wearing a back brace.

Jay town manager, Charlie Noonan, verified this incident,

as did state Senator Ed Irwin and his wife, state Representative Phyllis Irwin.

Tex came to Jay in 1979 as a boilermaker [from] a Chicago local for a job as a tank erector in the IP mill. He stayed after the job. Tex had been involved with drug rehab, especially for young people. He immediately became involved with the strike, and to the Jay strikers represented a true unionist opposed to the BE&K scabs. On one occasion the Wackenhut security people (goons) tried to force Tex's car off the road. Because of his southern drawl, he used his CB radio to cause havoc in the plant, like unloading wood where it should not be unloaded.

At the time of this interview (February 20, 1995), Tex said, "the company wins again. IP put it to us."

Also, Tex's wife made a union Tex doll for sale during the strike.

A Union Member's Wife and Proud of It!

Anonymous

I signed up to man the radio on the 3 to 7 A.M. shift. I'm now sitting here at 5 A.M. One guy just came in to picket from 5 to 9, otherwise no one was on the line. If it hadn't been for one other fella in the hall, who had been here since early morning the day before, I would have been alone. He stayed so I, an elderly woman, would not be here alone. To him, I owe my gratitude; to all of the others who are home sleeping and unconcerned, I feel contempt. A scab is a scab, but a union member who does not give of their time in this fight is a traitor. So you go to the meetings and sing the solidarity song, but where are you tonight? This is so sad it breaks my heart. If you believe in this thing, then be there when you're needed. I work full time and I'm here.

Bill has begged for help, the outreach members have told you you're needed, but it's been like a lot of other things, in one ear and out the other. Let Joe Blow do it. I'll help when it's convenient for me. I'll give when it doesn't hurt. I'm tired, Bill's tired, we're all tired, but that's not an excuse. Let's not have this thing break up on the inside. As President Kennedy said, "Ask not what the union can do for you, but what you can do for the union."

I'm going home now and sleep a few hours before I go to work. I'm tired, but I feel good about it. Can you say the same?

Letter of Resignation

Roy Bamford

November 21, 1988
Glen Zalkin
International Paper Company
Androscoggin Mill
Jay, Maine 04239

Glen Zalkin:

Because of International Paper's refusal to negotiate in good faith since early 1987; because of International Paper's refusal to continue premium Sunday pay (despite record profits); because of International Paper's refusal to recognize Christmas as a sacred day; because of International Paper's refusal to accept the fact that working men and women deserve to be treated with dignity; and because of International Paper's scab-loving, union-hating attitude—I find that it is not financially, emotionally, or socially necessary or feasible for me to return to such a rotten company!

Sincerely,
Roy Bamford
Former Employee

Labor unites to support UPIU in Jay. Over 8,000 people representing over 20 unions in New England march on the IP Androscoggin mill, August 1, 1987. Photo by Rene Brochu.

Epilogue

by
Jack Getman

The 1987 strike by Local 14 of the United Paperworkers International Union against the International Paper Company, in Jay, Maine, was one of the most dramatic and important episodes in modern U.S. labor history. It helped to convince organized labor that the traditional strike weapon was ineffective, led to a major effort to amend the National Labor Relations Act, and it signaled the demise of the system of adversarial collective bargaining that had dominated labor relations since World War II. For a time the strike invigorated the alliance between organized labor and Democratic party leaders, bringing to Jay national, state and local political leaders.

As is true of almost all important strikes today, it was the company, not the union, that was seeking concessions. International Paper Company had come to the bargaining table with a long list of demands, seeking to lower labor costs, to reduce jobs and to obtain greater managerial flexibility. When the union refused to give in to these demands and went on strike in protest, IP hired permanent replacement workers. Although the company had the advantage of enormous wealth and worldwide operations to compensate for lost production, the union fought an imaginative and effective battle. In many ways, the strike was a throwback to the 1930s, marked by enthusiastic rallies, effective alliances and grassroots activism.

Although the strike ended with a victory for the International Paper Company, it was a costly victory that convinced almost all of the other paper companies in the United States to reject IP's policies.

This book, with its firsthand recollections of the strike by those who took part, demonstrates that the cause of unionism still has the power to inspire workers to sacrifice and to create a sense of fellowship and solidarity among those involved in a common struggle. The testimonies serve to illustrate intelligence, sensitivity and unpretentious eloquence of working people fighting for a cause.

As the testimonies in this volume make clear, the strike permanently changed the lives of most of the participants and it fundamentally altered the community in which they live. The testimonies reflect the pain of loss and the bitterness of the strikers and their families toward:

- the International Paper Company—"Too proud to bargain with the Union" (Russell Brackett);

- the replacement workers—"The word hate took on a new meaning for me and that is what my feelings will always be" (Winnie Shink);

- the International Union—"The upper union echelon let Local 14 down. I hope there is a higher power that will some day make them pay their just dues" (Joan Fuller).

But even more pronounced are the feelings of pride, mutual affection and joy which the strike aroused in so many of those who took part. Bob Roy recalls how "it choked me up and . . . really made me feel good" when he presented a check to a Wednesday night meeting and the audience "broke into thunderous applause." Gloria Poulin recalls her feeling that "I had found family" during a trip to Colorado. Judy Willet recalls the "goose bumps that I felt and still feel every time I hear that song ('The Union Makes Us Strong!')." And the most frequently stated conclusion, "I would do the same thing all over again." In almost every testimony, one hears echoes of the solidarity that made this strike so moving an experience for the papermakers and their families.

So here's to the strikers at Jay and their families. You are right to feel angry and right to feel proud.

Chronology

A partial chronology of the 16-month strike at the International Paper Company's Androscoggin mill by 1,250 members of the United Paperworkers International Union Local 14 and the International Brotherhood of Firemen and Oilers Local 246:

1986	Paper companies meet and agree to go after concessions from the unions in contract negotiations across the country. International Paper Company, Boise Cascade Company and the Georgia Pacific Company lead the charge.
Oct. 29, 1986	International Paper Company President, Paul O'Neil, in a speech to the Maine Chamber of Commerce states that the company will be going after double time on Sunday in upcoming negotiations with union. They also want a lower tax rate, a decrease in the Workers Compensation rate and less environmental regulation.
Dec. 16, 1986	Local 14 offers IP a one-year contract extension. IP rejects the offer.
Feb. 1987	Union notifies IP they want to start contract negotiations. IP responds, wait until April.
March 20, 1987	UPIU tells IP it will utilize coordinated bargaining tactics against the company for refusing to

back off concessionary demands.

March 21, 1987	IP locks out 1,200 workers at its Mobile, Alabama, mill.
April 21, 1987	Contract negotiations begin. Union offers two-year extension. IP rejects.
May 4, 1987	First mass public meeting of the strike held. Larry Funk, chair of the Mobile, Alabama, negotiating committee, addresses the meeting.
May 31, 1987	Contracts between IP and the two unions expire.
June 4, 1987	The unions reject IP's contract offer and authorize the first strike at the Jay mill in more than 66 years. (98 percent of the membership vote, with 97 percent voting to strike.)
June 9, 1987	The unions reject IP's "final offer."
June 16, 1987	1,250 members of the two unions walk off the job and strike begins. Strikers rally at State House, the largest in 40 years.
June 24, 1987	First of 60 weekly mass meetings held during the strike, usually attended by over 1,000 people.
June 29, 1987	Scabs brought into mill.
July 2, 1987	First food bank distribution.
July 3, 1987	Veterans against IP hold first vigil.

July 7,
1987

Superior Court Justice signs an order limiting the number of union pickets at the mill to 12 per gate and barring union members from assembling on a road where the earlier confrontation had occurred.

July 10,
1987

235 scabs in mill.

July 17,
1987

470 scabs in mill.

July 19,
1987

UPIU announces plan to increase strike benefits from $55 a week to $200.

July 20,
1987

506 scabs in mill.

July 23,
1987

Selectmen nix $4.5 million bond for IP.

July 31,
1987

611 scabs in mill. Over half the work force is permanently replaced. IP sues union for $750,000.

Aug. 1,
1987

10,000 people rally and march in Jay to support strikers.

Aug. 3,
1987

Rally held in front of IP headquarters in Memphis, Tennessee.

Aug. 11,
1987

Environmental ordinances are adopted at a special Jay town meeting. IP files a lawsuit challenging the ordinances.

Aug. 12,
1987

UPIU President Wayne Glenn attends a weekly mass meeting. Glenn hails Local 14 in Jay as "a labor hero" and urges the rank and file to persevere. Strikers are eligible for unemployment benefits.

Aug. 22,   200 Jay workers attend rally in Lock Haven,
1987   Pennsylvania.

Aug. 24,   Delegations from Mobile, De Pere, Lock Haven
1987   and the UPIU meet with local leaders and mem-
               bers in Pine Bluff, Arkansas.

Sept. 1987   Hamilton, Ohio, locals get one-year contract ex-
               tension.

Sept. 6,   Thousands attend Labor Day rally in Waterville.
1987

Sept. 10,   IP offers double time at its Menasha, Wisconsin,
1987   mill.

Sept. 23,   Pine Bluff, Arkansas, locals vote to accept con-
1987   tract; major setback for striking locals.

Sept. 24,   Governor holds talks with union and IP.
1987

Sept. 28,   IP mill in Gardiner, Oregon, votes to strike.
1987

Sept. 29,   IP and union negotiators meet for nine minutes,
1987   adjourning without making progress toward set-
               tling the dispute. IP states that all but 100 work-
               ers have been permanently replaced.

Sept. 30,   Menasha, Wisconsin, mill votes to strike.
1987

Oct. 12,   At the mill, IP implements the contract rejected
1987   by the unions. Democratic presidential candidate
               Jesse Jackson attends a union rally in Jay for more
               than 3,500 strikers and their supporters.

Oct. 27,   OSHA fines IP $242,000.
1987

Oct. 30, 1987	Corinth, New York, mill rejects contract offer.
Nov. 21, 1987	More than 6,000 strikers and supporters rally and march to plant gate. U.S. Representative Richard Gephardt, then campaigning for the Democratic presidential nomination, addresses the crowd.
Nov. 23, 1987	Unions fined $10,000; held in contempt for July 7th injunction limiting pickets at the mill.
Nov. 24, 1987	The paperworkers' union announces it has hired labor leader Ray Rogers to lead a "corporate campaign."
Dec. 8 1987	Corinth mill accepts contract offer.
Dec. 16, 1987	Department of Environmental Protection fines IP $55,000 for August wastewater spill.
Dec. 17, 1987	Strikers launch a public appeal and announce plans to lead a caravan through New England to gain sympathy for their cause.
Jan. 28, 1988	Eight people are sent to the hospital following a hydrogen sulfide leak at IP.
Feb. 5, 1988	Nearly 4,000 residents of Jay and surrounding communities are forced to leave because of a 112,000-gallon chlorine dioxide leak at IP.
Feb. 14, 1988	Seven are injured in a chlorine leak at the mill.
Feb. 17, 1988	Governor John R. McKernan meets with IP Chairman John Georges in Portland to discuss safety at the mill in the aftermath of the leaks.

March 9, 1988	A group of top state officials, who inspected the mill following the February leaks, announce that they found no problems serious enough to warrant ordering the plant shut down.
March 28, 1988	IP and the unions open negotiations to establish a framework for settling labor disputes at the Jay mill and IP mills in three other states.
April 17, 1988	Strikers reject IP's latest proposal, throwing copies onto the floor of a meeting hall in Jay. The key provision would have given striking workers preferential hiring rights at four mills; the union insisted that the strikers get their jobs back.
April 30, 1988	More than 6,000 people march to the mill's gates to show support of the strike.
May 20, 1988	A replacement worker is killed when he is struck by fragments from a grinding wheel. The Occupational Safety and Health Administration (OSHA) begins an investigation.
June 6, 1988	Ticonderoga, New York, workers reject contract offer.
June 21, 1988	Jay voters authorize a $100,000 special appropriation to defend a new environmental ordinance enacted since the repeal of the ordinances that had been challenged by IP.
July 28, 1988	OSHA cites IP for hundreds of safety violations at the mill. IP agrees to pay more than $870,000 in fines.
Aug. 5, 1988	OSHA proposes $11,000 in fines stemming from the worker's death in May.
Aug. 11, 1988	Attorney General James E. Tierney files suit against IP in Superior Court, seeking fines for

violations of "virtually every environmental law."

Aug. 12, 1988
: UPIU national convention held in Las Vegas votes to do everything in its power to win the strikes.

Aug. 23, 1988
: Paperworkers charge that the strike has cost IP stockholders $284 million in losses.

Sept. 16, 1988
: Roving pickets hit Ticonderoga mill; workers stay out for half a day.

Sept. 26, 1988
: Jay selectmen approve a property tax reassessment for the mill for the first time in 12 years, pushing the mill's taxes up by about 15 percent, to $5.5 million a year.

Oct. 10, 1988
: The paperworkers union abruptly announces an end to strikes at IP mills in Jay and in Wisconsin and Pennsylvania.

Aug. 2, 1989
: IP fined $990,000 for violation of Clean Air Act and will install $5 million in pollution control equipment.

April 13, 1991
: IP fined $885,000 by state for past environmental violations.

Aug. 4, 1991
: IP found guilty on five Federal felony charges based on environmental violations and fined $2.2 million, second largest in U.S. history. Three weeks later, President George Bush appoints IP CEO John Georges to the Presidents Commission on Environmental Quality.

July 1992
: Local 14 is decertified by a vote of 616 to 361.

Number of strikers hired back by year. A number of these have
passed on, retired, been fired or have quit:

1988 - 12	1993 - 39
1989 - 115	1994 - 21
1990 - 104	1995 - 25
1991 - 70	1996 - 26
1992 - 72	1997 - 40

Honor Roll:
List of Strikers

List of people who struck the International Paper Company in Jay, Maine, for 16 months from June 16, 1987, until the strike was called off on October 10, 1988.

CHARLES ADAMS
RONALD ADAMS
STEVEN ADAMS
VERNON ADAMS
EUGENE ALLAIRE
DAVID ALLEN
EARL ALLEN
GENE ALLEN
LAWRENCE ALLEN
SHIRLEY ALLEN
TIMOTHY ALLEN
WILLIAM ALLEN
CHARLES ALLEN, JR.
GENE ALLEN, JR.
MARK AMERO
RICHARD AMERO
GILBERT ANDERS
MARCUS ARMANDI
GARY J. ARSENAULT
WAYNE ATWOOD
RICHARD AUCLAIR
ROGER AUDETTE
KELLEY AUSTIN
BRIAN BAKER
JOHN V. BALSAMO
VICTOR BALSAMO
HOWARD BAMFORD
ROY BAMFORD

FRED BARCLAY
TRUDY BARCLAY
MICHAEL BARKER
LOIS BARNETT
RICKIE BARNETT
WILLIAM BARRON
JAMES L. BARTASH
LINDON BARTLETT
JOHN BASTON
RICHARD BATES
BRENDA BEAULIEU
BRIAN BEAULIEU
JOHN BEAULIEU
LARRY BEAULIEU
GEORGE BECERRA
DAVID BECKLER
KENWOOD BECKLER
RONALD BECKLER
THOMAS BEECHUM
DAVID BEISAW
TERRY BELANGER
GILBERT BELLMORE
ROBERT L. BELYEA
RICHARD BENEDETTO
STEVEN BENEDETTO
CINDY BENNETT
JOEL BENSON
EMILE BERGERON

ALBERT BERNARD
GERARD BERNARD
LUCIEN (PETE) BER-
  NARD
STEVEN BERNARD
CLIFFORD BERRY
RANDALL BERRY
LARRY BESSEY
MARY BETTS
DANIEL BIBEAU
KATHI BIBEAU
PAUL BIBEAU
RANDALL BIBEAU
RENE BIBEAU
ELMER BICKFORD
LENDALL BICKFORD
MICHAEL BICKFORD
DWAYNE BILODEAU
GERARD BILODEAU
LAWRENCE BILODEAU
NORMAN R. BILODEAU
CONRAD BIZIER
ROGER BLAIS
ROGER BLAIS
BRUCE BLANCHARD
DAVID A. BLODGETT
STEPHEN BLODGETT
OLIVER BLOOD, JR.

SIMONE BLOUIN
ARMAND BOIVIN
BERNARD BOIVIN
DOUGLAS BOIVIN
GREGG BOIVIN
LOUIS BOIVIN
PHILIP BOIVIN
RANDALL BOIVIN
ROBERT BOIVIN
WILFRED BOND
BRUCE BONNEVIE
RICHARD BONNEVIE
DEBRA BOOTHBY
ARTHUR BOUCHARD, JR.
PAUL B. BOUCHER
GERARD BOURASSA
JAMES A. BOUTHAT
WENDELL BOUTWELL
JOSEPH L. BOWEN
ROBERT BOYLE
ARTHUR BRACKETT
MALCOLM BRACKETT
RUSSELL BRACKETT
DONNA BRAULT
EDWARD BRAULT
JANICE BRELSFORD
GERARD BRETON
JODY BRETON
LAURENCE BRETON
ROBERT BRETON
KENNETH BREWER
HENRY BRIMIGION
DANIEL BROCHU
GERARD BROCHU
JAMES BROCHU
RENE BROCHU
THOMAS BROOKS
DANIEL BROUGHAM
WILLIAM BROUGHAM
ALTON BROWN
STANLEY BROWN
ROBERT BRUNDAGE, JR.
CLARENCE BRYANT
CLINTON BRYANT
DAVID BRYANT
DONALD BRYANT
FLORENCE BRYANT
KERMIT BRYANT
LARRY BRYANT
NANCY BRYANT
NORMAN BRYANT
PETER BRYANT
ROBERT BRYANT
WARREN BRYANT

ARNOLD BUCK
JAMES BUCK
DALE BUCKINGHAM
DOMINIC J. BUDZKO II
VIVIAN BUKER
MICHAEL BUOTE
RUDOLPH BUOTE
ALMONT BURBANK
HOWARD BURHOE
BRENDA BURKE
EDWARD BURKE
JACK BURKE
DAVID BURNHAM
MICHAEL S. BURNS
JOEL BUSHIE, JR.
GEORGE BUSSIERE
RICHARD BUSSIERE
ROGER CADRIN
BARRY CAMPBELL
TERRY CAMPBELL
BRENDA L. CAPTAIN
GENE CASEY
JOHN CASEY
JOSEPH CASTANEDA
ADELARD CASTONGUAY
ALEC CASTONGUAY
ANDRE CASTONGUAY
CHARLES CASTONGUAY
DENIS CASTONGUAY
GEORGE CASTONGUAY
JOSEPH CASTONGUAY
MARCEL CASTONGUAY
PAUL CASTONGUAY
RENE CASTONGUAY
THOMAS CASTONGUAY
RANDALL CHAISSON
WALTER CHANCE, JR.
BARRY CHANDLER
ROBERT CHAPPELL
RAYMOND CHAREST
ARTHUR CHASE
EAN CHEA
NORBERT CHESSIE
ARMAND CHICOINE
CLARENCE CHICOINE
LAWRENCE CHICOINE
LAWRENCE CHICOINE,
   JR.
LOUIS CHICOINE
ROBERT CHICOINE
LEONARD CHILDRESS
JOHN CHOUINARD, JR.
ALBERT CHRETIEN
PAUL CHRETIEN

PHILIP CHRETIEN
REGINALD CHRETIEN
RICHARD CHURCHILL
JAMES CIESLAK
WILLIAM H. CLARDY
BRUCE WATSON CLARK
BRUCE WAYNE CLARK
DONALD CLARK
LYNDON CLARK
MATHEW CLARK
DEREK COBB
STACY COBB
ROBERT COFFMAN
JERRY COLLINS
LAWRENCE COLLINS
RICHARD COLLINS
MICHAEL COLLINS, JR.
RALPH CONANT
RICHARD CONWAY
ALAN COOK
BYRON COOK
DAVID COOK
FLOYD COOK
HERBERT COOK
REGINALD COOK
RICHARD COOK
NELSON COOLIDGE
CLINTON COOLIDGE, JR.
JUDITH COOMBS
DANNY CORCORAN
ROBERT CORCORAN
RANDI CORNELIO
THOMAS CORNELIO
DANIEL COTE
JAMES COTE
MICHAEL COTE
THOMAS COTE
WON COUILLARD
ROBERT COULOMBE
AURELIEN COUTURE
DARRYL COUTURE
DEBRA COUTURE
DENNIS COUTURE
GILLES COUTURE
KRISTI J. COUTURE
MARK COUTURE
RONALD J. COUTURE
RONALD L. COUTURE
CHARLES CRAFTS
BARRY CROMMETT
LEE CRONKHITE
LEROY CRONKHITE
DUANE CROSBY
JOHN CROSSON

MICHAEL CROSSON
JOHN CROWLEY
RALPH CUNLIFFE
LINWOOD CURRIER
PATRICIA CURRIER
SARAH CURTIS
SHERMAN CURTIS
WALTER F. CURTIS
CLINTON CUSHMAN, JR.
JOSEPH CYR
DONALD DAIGLE
RICHARD DALESSAN-
  DRO
FRANK DALESSANDRO,
  JR.
RICHARD DALESSAN-
  DRO, JR.
SUSAN DALRYMPLE
RICHARD DAMON, JR.
ERIC O. DASHIELL
DAVID DAVIS
KATHLEEN DAVIS
RICHARD M. DAVIS
STEPHEN DAVIS
VERNON DAVIS, JR.
BRUCE DAVIS, SR.
LESTER M. DEANE
ROBERT DEANE
STEVEN DEANE
DEBRA DECKER
DERICK DECKER
MARK DECKER
RONDELL DEERING
ROBERT DEGONE
STEVEN DEGONE
RAYMOND DELISLE
RODNEY DEMERS
ANTHONY DEMILLO
SANTO DEMILLO
FRANK DEMING
ROY DEMING, JR.
JOHN DEMORAS
PAUL DENTON
CAROL DESJARDINS
DAVID DESJARDINS
DENNIS DESJARDINS
GARY DESJARDINS
JAMES DESJARDINS
RAYMOND DESJARDINS
RICHARD DESJARDINS
PHILIP DESOTTO
PAUL DESPRES
SHERRY DIAZ
ROBERT DICKSON

ALEX DION
DAVID DION
FREDDIE DIPOMPO
R. NELSON DIPOMPO,
  JR.
JOHN DISOTTO
HENRY DISOTTO, JR.
DOUGLAS DOIRON
EDWARD DOIRON
NORMAN DOIRON
PETER DOIRON
ROBERT DOIRON
SHAWN DOIRON
STEVEN DOIRON
JAMES DONALD
JOHN DONALD
WARREN DOREY
ROBERT DOUCETTE
BRIAN DOUGHTY
PETER DRAPER
WILLIAM DRINKWATER
JACK DRISCOLL
JOHN W. DRISCOLL
STEPHEN DRUMMOND
WILLIAM DUBE
WILLIE V. DUBE
WAYNE DUBOIS
JOSEPH DUBORD, JR.
MICHAEL DUCHENEY
RANDY DWELL
RONALD DUFOUR
ROSE DUFOUR
ALFRED DUFOUR, JR.
EDMUND DUGUAY
LAWRENCE DUGUAY
MAURICE DUGUAY
CHRISTOPHER DUMAIS,
  SR.
JAMES DUNHAM
RICHARD DUPONT
JIM DWINAL
HAROLD DWYER
RICHARD DYER
BRUCE DYKE
BRUCE EASTMAN
PHILIP EDWARDS
NEIL ELLIS
CHARLES ELLIS, JR.
RICHARD ELWELL
OSCAR EMMONS
STEVEN ESTY
SCOTT A. FAIRBANKS
PAUL FARMER
LARRY FARNUM

LINWOOD FARRELL
ALAN FARRINGTON
BERT FARRINGTON
BRUCE FARRINGTON
CHUN FARRINGTON
DEAN FARRINGTON
MAYNARD FARRINGTON
MILTON FARRINGTON
ROBERT FARRINGTON
RONALD FARRINGTON
SCOTT FARRINGTON
GREGORY P. FERGOLA
DOUGLAS W. FERLAND
RICHARD FERLAND
ROGER FERLAND
EDWARD FIELD
DANIEL FINLEY
JAMES FINLEY
STANLEY FISH
EARLE FLAGG
FORREST FLAGG
JOHN FLAGG
JULIE FLAGG
ROBERT FLANDERS
TIMOTHY FLYNN
DUANE FOLSOM
JAMES FORBES
TORY N. FORD
VERNON FORD
PAUL FORTIER
ROMEO FORTIER
GLENN FOSTER
BRUCE FOURNIER
DEBRA FOURNIER
GERHARD FOURNIER
JOHN FOURNIER
JOSEPH FOURNIER
LIONEL FOURNIER
RAYMOND FOURNIER
RICHARD FOURNIER
ROGER FOURNIER
ROGER J. FOURNIER
THOMAS FOURNIER
TIMOTHY FOURNIER
FREDERICO FRAN-
  CHETTI
HEIDI L. FRANCHETTI
KEVIN FRANCHETTI
FREDERICO FRAN-
  CHETTI, JR
KENNETH FRANZOSE
RICHARD FRAZIER
DONALD FRECHETTE
JOSEPH FRECHETTE

MARK FRECHETTE
GARY FRENCH
LLOYD FRENCH
KATHERINE FREY
RALPH FRIEND
EARL FULLER
ERIC FULLER
CHARLES H. FULLERTON
LAWRENCE GAGNE
FRANCIS GAGNON
PAUL GAGNON
CRAIG GALOUCH
LINDA GAMMON
ROLAND GAMMON
JOHN GARDNER
ROBERT GARLAND
EDWARD GATCHELL
JOE GATS
WILLIAM GATS
RICHARD GAUTHIER
YOLAND GAWIN
BRENT GAY
VONITA GERRIER
BRYAN GERRY
JOHN GIBBS
RICHARD GIBBS
ALBERT GILBERT
EUGENE GILBERT
JAMES GILBERT
JEFFREY GILBERT
LINDA GILBERT
PIERRE GILBERT
GREGORY GILL
BERT GIVEN
MARK GLOVER
SHAWN GOODROW
WAYNE GOODWIN
DENNIS GOSSELIN
RAYMOND GOSSELIN
CHESTER GOULD
EMERSON GOULD
NORMAN GOULD
RAYMOND GOULD
STEPHEN GOULD
NANCY GOULETTE
CASWELL GRAY
RICHARD GRAY
ROBERT GRAY
ROBERT R. GRAY
CLAYTON GREELEY
STFPHEN GREELEY
JOAN L. GREENLEAF
LEE STEPHEN GREEN-
    LEAF

MICHAEL GREENLEAF
RONALD GREENLEAF
FRANK GREENWOOD
MARCO GRIMALDI
ALAN GRONDIN
DANIEL GRONDIN
GASTON GRONDIN
JOSEPH GROOMES, JR.
DAVID GROVER
GEORGE GROVER
WILLIS GROVER
ROBERT GROVES
RAYMOND GUEST
RICHARD GUILD
WAYNE HACHEY
JOHN HAGERSTROM
ROBERT HALEY
CARL HALL
ROBERT HALL
JAMES HALLIDAY, SR.
RUSSELL HALLOWELL
MAUREEN HAMBLIN
CHRISTOPHER HAMIL-
    TON
THOMAS HAMLIN
BARRY HAMMOND
STEPHEN HAMNER
DALE HARDY
PAMELA A. HARDY
WILLIAM HARDY
CHARLES HARKINS, III
TIMOTHY HARKNESS
DEAN HARLOW
WILLIAM HARLOW
CHESTER HARRIS
ROBERT HARRIS
KELLEE HART
REBECCA HART
MICHAEL HARTFORD
GERALDINE HARVELL
RICHARD HARVELL
LAWRENCE HARVIE
RANDY HASTINGS
DUANE HATHAWAY
BERNARD HATHAWAY,
    JR.
LARRY HEALD
RICHARD HEALD
LUCIA HEALEY
DONNA HEBERT
JEFFREY HEBERT
KEVIN HEBERT
DAVID HEIRD
JAMES HEIRD

WALTER HEMINGWAY
CONRAD HENNESSY
DAVID HENRY
GARY HENRY
LARRY HENRY
MARY HENRY
OSWALD HENRY
OVILA HENRY
PRISCILIEN HENRY
ROGER HENRY
THOMAS HERSEY
BERTRAND HEUTZ
HARRISON HICKS
HARRY HIGGINS
PHILIP HILL
JAMES HILTON
CLAYTON HILTZ
GARY HILTZ
RAYMOND HILTZ, JR.
ALVIN HISCOCK
BRIAN HISCOCK
LEANDER HISCOCK
LEROY HISCOCK
ROBERT HISCOCK
STEPHEN HISCOCK
TIMOTHY E. HISCOCK
TY NGOC HO
MICHAEL HOBBS
WILLIAM G. HODGKINS
WILLIAM S. HODGKINS
WAYNE HOFFMAN
DANIEL HOGAN
TERRENCE HOGAN
ARTHUR HOLMAN
MARSHALL HOLMAN
DANIEL HOLT
MELVILLE HOOD, III
LEWIS HORTON
GARY HOULE
MICHAEL HOULIHAN
RICHARD HOWATT
DAVID E. HOWES
KENNETH HOWES
JACK HOYT
RUSSELL HUBBARD
CHARLIE HUFF, JR.
NELSON HURD
VINTON HUTCHINS
DAVID HUTCHINSON
DELMONT HUTCHINSON
JAN HUTCHINSON
STEPHEN B. HUTCHIN-
    SON
LESTER HUTCHINSON,
    JR.

KENNETH IMLAY
JAMES B. IRISH
WILMONT IRISH
BERCHARD JACKMAN
RICHARD S. JACKSON
WILLIAM JACOBS
BERNARD JACQUES
FELIX JACQUES
JAMES K. JACQUES
JAMES R. JACQUES
ROBERT JACQUES
SHARON JACQUES
WILFRED JACQUES, JR.
CHARLES JAMES
GARY JASKALEN
DANA JASMIN
RODNEY JENNINGS
KENNETH JERRY
KEVIN JEWETT
MARVIN JEWETT
RANDALL JEWETT
HAROLD JOHNSON, III
GERARD JOLICOEUR
JOHN JOLICOEUR
GEORGE JONES
GORDON JONES
LOUIS JONES
LUANNE JONES
ROBERT JONES
RONALD JONES
TREBY JONES
GENE JORDAN
JAMES JORDAN
KENNETH JUDD
LAURENCE JUDD
RAYMOND JUDD
THOMAS JUDD
JIM KACKNOVICH
DANIEL KANE
BRIAN KARKOS
JEFFREY KEMP
RICHARD KEMP
RICKY KEMP
DEBORAH KEMPTON
DAVID KENDALL
FRANK KENDALL
JOSEPHINE KENDALL
CHARLES KENNEDY
JOHN H. KENNEDY
ROCKWOOD KENNEDY
CHARLES M. KENNEDY,
    JR.
JAMES KENNISON
SAMUEL KITTREDGE

RICHARD KNAPP
HAROLD KNOCKWOOD
WAYNE KNOWLTON
GERALD KNOX
LINDA KONDAS
BRIAN KORHONEN
RICHARD KORHONEN
RONALD KORHONEN
MARGO KYES
ROBERT L'ITALIEN
DONALD LABBE
GARY LABBE
JOEL J. LABBE
NEIL LABBE
RANDY LABBE
RENE LABBE
WAYNE LABBE
LAWRENCE LABRECQUE
MICHAEL LABRECQUE
PETER LABRECQUE
ROBERT LABRECQUE
DAVID LACHAPELLE
JONATHAN LADD
BERNAL LAKE
CAROL LAKE
THOMAS LAKE
WALTER LAKE
NORMAND LALIBERTE
JOHN E. LAMAY
GEORGE LAMB
JEFFREY P. LAMB
PETER LAMBERT
JOSEPH LANDRY
KEVIN LANDRY
MARTIN P. LANDRY
JOSEPH LANGLAIS
BERNARD LANOLIN
DAVID LAPLANTE
EMILE LAPLANTE
RAOUL LAPLANTE
ROBERT LAPLANTE
ROBERT LAVERDIERE
ROGER LAVERDIERE
GEORGE LAVOIE
RICHARD D. LEACH
CHARLES LEADBETTER
CHARLES F. LEADBET-
    TER, JR.
CECIL LEAVITT
RUTH B. LEBEL
DALE R. LEBLANC
RENE J. LEBLANC
RONALD LEBLANC
FRANK LECLAIR

NORM R. LECLAIR
MARK LECLERC
RONALD LECLERC
DENNIS LEE
ERLON LEE
ROGER LEE
PHILIPPE LEGER
DANIEL LEGERE
FRED LEGERE
MATHIAS LEGERE
MICHAEL LEGERE
PETER LEGERE
HENRY LERETTE
RAYMOND R. LESSARD
NORMAN LETALIEN
MARC A. LETENDRE
ARTHUR LETOURNEAU
DAVID LEWIS
ALAN LIBBY
FELIX A. LIBBY
JEFFERY LIBBY
PHILLIP LIBERTY
STEPHEN LINCOLN
RONALD LINDHOLM
MICHAEL LITTLE
GEORGE LITTLEFIELD
WILLIAM LLOYD
JAMES LOMBARD
DARREL LONG
JOSEPH LONGLEY
ROBERT LOON, JR.
MAITLAND LORD
MAITLAND LORD, JR.
JAMES LOSEY
KENNETH LOTHROP
HAROLD LOVEJOY, JR.
DARREN LOVEWELL
DAVID LOVEWELL
ROBBIE LUCARELLI
PHYLLIS LUCK
JOHN LUCIANO
MICHAEL LUCIANO
JAMES LYMAN
ANDREW LYNCH
DAVID MADISON
ANGELA MAGOON
JEFF MARCEAU
PAUL MARCEAU
RALPH MARCEAU
JO MARCHETTI
MARTIN MARCHETTI
RALPH MARCHETTI
RONALD MARCHETTI
VINCENT MARCHETTI

LOUIS MARCHETTI, JR.
ARMAND MARCOTTE
STEVEN MARCOTTE
ANDRE MARICHAL
CAROL MARINO
ROBERT MARINO
DONALD MARQUIS
KIM MARSHALL
LYNNE MARSHALL
RONALD MARSTERS
BRUCE L. MARTIN
CHARLES MARTIN
JOHN MARTIN
MATTHEW MARTIN
JOHN MASTINE
RUSSELL MATHERS, II
ROBERT MAXWELL
DAVID McANINCH
RONALD McCARTHY
DAVID McCLUSKEY
GREGORY McCOURT
LEE McDANIEL
LLOYD McDANIEL
BARRY McDONALD
BRENT McDONALD
BRIAN McDONALD
CARROLL McDONALD
CLOVIS McDONALD
DOUGLAS McDONALD
EARL McDONALD
JEFFREY McDONALD
KATHLEEN McDONALD
OLIN McDONALD
SHERYL McDONALD
VERNON McDONALD
ROBERT McDONALD, SR.
WALTER J. McDOUGALL,
    JR.
RICHARD McGINTY
GARY McGRANE
ROBERT McLAIN
RICHARD H. McPHER-
    SON
MAURICE MELANSON
EDWARD MELCHER
LINDA MERCHANT
DAVID MERCIER
DOUGLAS MERRILL
OLIVE MERRILL
ROBERT MERRILL
GLEN MERROW
WILLIAM J. MESERVE
WILLIAM R. MESERVE
ROBERT METCALF

ARMAND METIVIER
MAURICE METIVIER
EARL MILLER
PAUL MILLER
CHARLES MILLER, JR.
DAVID MILLS
LELAND MINGO
GARY MITCHELL
LEROY MONROE
RICHARD MOODY
PAUL MOORE
DANIEL MOREAU
MAURICE MOREAU
GAIL MORGAN
BERTRAND MORIN
RAYMOND MORRELL
LINWOOD MORSE
BRUCE MOULTON
JAMES E. MURPHY
MARTIN NADEAU
MICHAEL NADEAU
MOHAMMAD NADERI
KEVIN NASATOWICZ
MARK NASON
FRANCIS NELKE
DONALD NELSON
MICHAEL NELSON
RICHARD NELSON
JAMES NEUSCHWAN-
    GER
BEVERLY NEWCOMB
JOHN NEWCOMB
DANNY NEWCOMBE
BRIAN NEWELL
DENNIS NEWTON
MICHAEL NEWTON
DENNIS NICHOLS
FRANKLIN NICHOLS
WILLIAM NICHOLS
EDWARD NICKERSON
CHARLES E. NIEDNER
MARK NIEDNER
RICHARD NILE
GERARD NOLETTE
DUANE NORRIS
WILLIAM S. NORRIS
CLIFTON NORTON
PHILIP NORTON
WILFRED NOYES
DENNIS OBERTON
RELLAND ODONAL
DOUGLAS OLIVER
MALCOLM ORFF
RHONDA ORFF

MICAH OSGOOD
GERALD OUELLETTE
JACK OUELLETTE
JAMES OUELLETTE
JEAN OUELLETTE
LAURIER OUELLETTE
NORMAND OUELLETTE
PATRICIA OUELLETT E
RAYMOND OUELLETTE
STEPHEN OUELLETTE
THOMAS OUELLETTE
KENNETH PAGE
FRANCIS PALING
DANIEL PALMER
RICHARD PARADIS
PAUL L. PARENT
LOUISE PARKER
WAYNE PARKER
RICHARD PATNAUDE
JEFFREY S. PAYEUR
ADOLPHE PAYEUR, JR.
NORMAN PEASE
JOHN R. PELLETIER
PETER PELLETIER
RICHARD PELLETIER
RAMON PEREZ
DOROTHY PERKINS
DEREK PERREAULT
MAURICE PERREAULT
ROBERT PERREAULT
ROGER PERREAULT
TIMOTHY PERREAULT
ROBERT PERRON
BRIAN PERRY
LUTHER PERRY
MICHAEL W. PERRY
GARY PETTENGILL
MICHAEL PHELAN
MAURICE PHILIPPON
FRANCIS PICARD
GEORGE PILLSBURY
DONALD PINEAU
MICHAEL PINEAU
RAYMOND PINEAU
WAYNE PIPER
FRANK PLAISTED
GEORGE PLAISTED
JOSEPH PLANTE
ROGER PLANTE
THERESA PLOURDE
THOMAS PLOURDE
OWEN PLUMMER
JOSEPH POISSON
RUSSELL POLAND

GERALD POMELOW
CRAIG POMERLEAU
JOSEPH POMERLEAU
NORMAN POMERLEAU
HAROLD POMERLEAU, JR.
DONALD POMEROY
MARK POMEROY
PAULETTE POOLE
CHARLES POSIK
JAMES POSIK
DANIEL POULIN
DAVID POULIN
ERNEST POULIN
LAURIER POULIN
MARCEL POULIN
MARK POULIN
MAURICE POULIN
RAYMOND POULIN
DAVID POWELL
JOHN G. POWER
RICHARD PRATT
THOMAS PRATT
OLIVIA PRESBY
ROGER PRESBY
WILLIAM PRESSEY
JAMES PURINGTON
LARRY PURINGTON
MICHAEL PURRINGTON
ROSS PURRINGTON
CLAYTON PUTNAM
LINTON QUIRRION
LINTON A. QUIRRION
FRED QUIRRION, JR.
HERSCHEL RACKLIFF
HERSCHEL RACKLIFF, JR.
DONALD RALPH, JR.
BRYON RAMSDELL
DANIEL RAND
CLARIS RANGER
CLIFFORD RANGER
JOHN RANGER, JR.
ARTHUR RAYMOND
JOSEPH RAYMOND
LORRAINE REAL
HAROLD REDMAN, JR.
ALLEN REED
ANATOLE RICHARD
DARREN RICHARD
DAVID RICHARD
DIANE RICHARD
DONALD RICHARD
EMILE RICHARD

GEORGE RICHARD
JAMES RICHARD
JEAN RICHARD
RANDALL RICHARD
RAYMOND RICHARD
ALBERT RICHARDS
ANNETTE RICHARDS
ARTHUR RICHARDS
GERARD RICHARDS
JACK R. RICHARDS
JEFFREY RICHARDS
PETER RICHARDS
RANDY RICHARDS
ROBERT RICHARDS
LESLIE RICHARDSON
FLOYD RICHMOND
ROBERT RICHMOND
THOMAS RICHMOND
DONNA T. RICKARDS
ROBERT RICKARDS
DALE RIORDAN
JOHN (PETER) RIORDAN
TIMOTHY ROBBINS
YOLANDA ROBBINS
ROBIN ROBERTS
WILLIAM ROBERTS
CLINTON ROBINSON
GLEN ROBINSON
JERRY ROBINSON
PERLEY ROBINSON
RICHARD ROBINSON
SANDRA ROBINSON
WILLIAM ROBINSON
LINWOOD ROLFE
RICHARD ROMANO
ALLEN ROWE
BERNARD ROY
GREGORY ROY
MAURICE ROY
MICHAEL ROY
RAOUL ROY
RAYMOND ROY
RICHARD ROY
ROBERT ROY
ROGER ROY
ROLAND ROY
RONALD ROY
RONALD C. ROY
WAYNE ROY
WILFRED ROY
RICHARD RUSH, JR.
LAWRENCE RUSSELL
JAMES RYDER
ROLAND SAMSON

GERARD SAMSON, JR.
CHARLES SANBORN
WAYNE SAPIEL
JOHN SCAPPATICCI
ROBERT SCHERPF
LINDA SCHOFIELD
MICHELE SCOTT
JAY SCRIBNER
TIMOTHY SEELOW
RICHARD SHAFFER
BERNARD SHINK
JOSEPH SHINK
MARCEL SHINK
DEAN SIDNEY
JAYE SIMONEAU
LEO SIMONEAU
RICHARD SIMONEAU
NEREE SIMONEAU, JR.
RUSSELL SIMPSON
BONNIE SLOAN
PAUL SLOVAK
PAULINE SLOVAK
THOMAS SLOVAK
DONNA SMALL
ALBERT SMALL, III
BAYNE SMITH
CHRISTOPHER SMITH
DAVID SMITH
DAVID O. SMITH
DONALD SMITH
DOUGLAS SMITH
ELIZABETH SMITH
HORACE SMITH
LINDA SMITH
LORRAINE SMITH
NORRIS SMITH
NORRIS SMITH
RICHARD SMITH
TERRY SMITH
WESLEY SMITH
CLARK SOOTHER
JOLINE SOOTHER
LISA SOOTHER
RANDALL J. SOOTHER
RONALD SOOTHER
WILBUR SOOTHER
WILLIAM SPILLER
MICHAEL SPIOTTA
RICHARD SPROUL
TEDDY SPYDELL
CHARLENE ST. PIERRE
GEORGE ST. PIERRE
ROBERT ST. PIERRE
LINDA STANHOPE

STANTON STANHOPE
GRAYDON STANHOPE, JR.
GORDON STANLEY
RODNEY STANLEY
RODNEY STAPLES
LYNN STERRY, JR.
BRUCE STEVENS
CHRIS STEVENS
WILLIAM STEWART
JAMES STEWART, JR.
HOWARD STIMANS
ARTHUR STORER
TERRY STORER
CARL STOWE, JR.
DAVID STROUT
ROBERT STROUT
ELLEN STURTEVANT
ROYAL SWAN
ALAN A. SWETT
REG TARDIF
RICHARD TARDIF
GEORGE TAYLOR
MELODY TENNEY
CHARLES THAYER
BARRY THERRIEN
CAROL THERRIEN
GERALD THERRIEN
NORMAN THERRIEN
RICHARD THERRIEN
RODNEY THERRIEN
WILLIAM THERRIEN
BARBARA THIBEAU
VALMOND THIBODEAU
ARTHUR THOMAS
BRYCE THOMAS
ROBERT THOMPSON
MARTIN THORNE
CHARLES TIDSWELL, JR.
LINDA TILTON
CHRYSTAL TIMBERLAKE
DEBRA TIMBERLAKE
JOHN TIMBERLAKE
KENNETH TIMBERLAKE
MICHAEL TIMBERLAKE
RENDA TIMBERLAKE

ROBERT TIMBERLAKE
ROLAND TIMBERLAKE
VICKI TIMBERLAKE
EDWARD TOBIN
GERALD TOOTHAKER, JR.
ROBIN TOWLE
RICHARD TRACY
TERRY TRASK
TOM TRASK
MICHAEL TRIPP
WALLACE TRIPP
WILLIS TRIPP
PHILIP TRYON
BRUCE TURCOTTE
GUY TURMEL
ARTHUR TYLER
CALVIN TYLER
THOMAS VALLEY
DALE VARNEY
MAYNARD VEINOTTE
JEFFREY VIENNEAU
TERRANCE VIGNEAULT
RODNEY VINING
CONNIE VIOLETTE
DOUGLAS VIOLETTE
RICHARD VOTER, JR.
MEREDITH WAITE
STEPHEN WAITE
ADRIAN WAITE, JR.
DEBORAH WALKER
TOM WALKER
JOHN WALP
GEORGE WALSH
GERALD WALSH
DAVID WARD
KEN WARD
CALVIN WARDWELL
JUDITH WARDWELL
DWIGHT WATSON
EUGENE WEED
WILSON WEED
CLIFFORD WELCH
PERCY WELCH
ROBERT WELCH
WENDY WELCH

JOSEPH WESTON
SHARON WESTON
AVARD WHEELER
CHARLES WHEELER
MEDLEY WHEELER
WILLIAM WHEELER
RONALD WHETZEL
ALBERT WHITE
BRIAN WHITE
BRIGITTE WHITE
DANIEL L. WHITE
DELANCE WHITE
LINDA WHITE
STEVEN WHITE
TERRY M. WHITE
WAYNE WHITEHOUSE
JAMES WHITTEMORE
MARSHA WHITTEMORE
DOUGLAS WIGGINS
GERALD WIGHT
ROBERT WIGHT
RICHARD WILCOX
SUSAN WILKINS
GARY WILLETT
LOUIS WILLETT, III
JANET WILLIAMS
RICHARD WILLS
WALTER WILLS
FREDERICK WILSON
RONALD WING
WENDY J. WING
DARRYL WINTER
MARK E. WITHERELL
GARY WOODCOCK
JAMES YAHN
HOWARD YEATON, JR.
STEVEN YEATON
CASSIUS YORK
CLYDE YOUNG
EARL YOUNG
JAMES YOUNG
LEONARD YOUNG
THOMAS YOUNG
WILLIAM BARRON
RON BECKLER
WENDELL BOUTWELL

Members Now Deceased

ROBERT BRETON
DANIEL BROUGHAM
BARRY CAMPBELL
ARMAND CHICOINE
ALAN COOK
LEE CRONKHITE
RALPH CUNLIFFE
JAMES DUNHAM
RICHARD DYER
RICHARD ELWELL
OSCAR EMMONS
RONALD FARRINGTON
ROGER FOURNIER
RALPH FRIEND
PAUL GAGON
EDWARD GETCHELL
WAYNE GOODWIN
ROBERT HARRIS
EDWARD HASTINGS

TERRY HOGAN
ROCKWOOD KENNEDY
RONALD KORHONEN
WALTER LAKE
JO MARCHETTI
RALPH MARCHETTI
LOUIS MARCHETTI, JR.
PAUL MILLER
LINWOOD MORSE
GERALD NOLETTE
TOM PLOURDE
OWEN PLUMMER
RAYMOND POULIN
ROGER PRESBY
ARTHUR RAYMOND
BRYCE THOMAS
JOHN TIMBERLAKE
LINDA WHITE
GERALD WIGHT

Besides these strikers, there are a number of scabs and super scabs who died since June 16, 1987. There were no board members of the International Paper Company who suffered at all because of the strike.

Resources

Information about the strike can be found at:

- Special Collections Department, Fogler Library, University of Maine, Orono, Maine. The Kellman Papers (Jay Strike Collection) includes computerized index, video index and thousands of newspaper articles, letters, interviews, paperworker historical documents, internal organizing papers and more.

- Local 14 Union Hall, Jay, Maine.

- Northeast Historic Films, Bucksport, Maine, houses a collection of video tapes made during the strike. It includes tape of the 60 mass meetings held during the strike, television news reports, demonstrations and films made about the strike. The collection includes a computer index.

- Bureau of Labor Education, University of Maine, Orono, Maine.